Joseph

Joseph

A Gateway to the LORD

Merrell M. Peters

WIPF & STOCK · Eugene, Oregon

JOSEPH
A Gateway to the Lord

Wipf & Stock
An Imprint of Wipf and Stock Publishers
199 W. 8th Ave., Suite 3
Eugene, OR 97401

www.wipfandstock.com

PAPERBACK ISBN: 978-1-5326-3937-1
HARDCOVER ISBN: 978-1-5326-3938-8
EBOOK ISBN: 978-1-5326-3939-5

Dedication

For Anne C. Russell, my wife

When her glance, ". . . sparkled o'er aught that was bright in my story,/ I knew it was love and felt it was glory."

Contents

Acknowledgements

I FIRST HEARD THE story of Joseph and his brothers read to me as a young child by my mother, Elizabeth Peters, out of Hurlburt's *Story of the Bible*. My mother died at age 102 while this book was being prepared. Even as she became increasingly frail, her encouragement for my studies never flagged.

My Hebrew studies started when I was age 63 with the Hebrew Reading Crash Course, a project of the National Jewish Outreach Center. The course was offered at the Jewish Community Center in Saint Paul, Minnesota, whose tagline is: "You belong here." The tag is true, I always feel welcome at the "J."

The reading course was taught by Rabbi David Fredman, Aish Minnesota's Executive Director. He made the difficult task of recognizing and pronouncing Hebrew words most pleasant. I would encourage anyone interested in the Hebrew language to start with the crash course. Rabbi Fredman was very disciplined in focusing on Hebrew letters. He did not discuss Hebrew grammar. Once, however, he deviated from this principle and pointed out how the same Hebrew word was translated differently in two verses. Understanding both concepts expanded the meaning of the verses.

I had never heard an argument like this where the Hebrew language shifted the meaning of Scripture verses. I decided to pursue my study of Hebrew further. Most Lutheran pastors are required to take Hebrew in order to qualify for ordination. This fact led me to the website of Luther Seminary in Saint Paul, but I had difficulty navigating it. I wrote to the Help Desk at the seminary asking whether I could take a beginning Hebrew class. My past experience with other help desks suggested little hope that I would receive an answer.

But lo and behold, a seminary student sitting in a small office in the basement of the Seminary's oldest building responded and passed my request forward. This led to my email correspondence with Ms Sandy Hammerlind, Associate in Ministry for Admissions. Semester after semester, Ms Hammerlind guided me through the registration process. Truly, but for the kindness of the Help Desk personnel and Ms Hammerlind, I would have surrendered any hope of studying Hebrew.

In the summer of 2014, I took a concentrated course in Basic Hebrew, three hours a day, five days a week, for six weeks. The course was taught by Dr. Mark A Throntveit, Elsa B Lovell Professor of Old Testament. I knew nothing of Dr. Throntveit until he charged into the classroom full of enthusiasm for the Hebrew language. Luther Seminary turned out to be a wonderful place to study Hebrew. The courses were taught by Dr. Throntveit, the head of the Old Testament Department. This beginner got to work directly with the expert. Over four semesters, I took courses, did the homework, took the tests, and wrote the papers. I decided even if I was just auditing the classes, I would do the work Dr. Throntveit requested. Any facility I have with Hebrew, which I admit is most limited, is the result of Dr. Throntveit's generous teaching and encouragement. He has been teaching Basic Hebrew for over 30 years. It takes real commitment to have enthusiasm for beginning language students after hearing the same mistakes repeated year after year. Dr Throntveit opened a whole world of Hebrew studies to me and I remain most grateful for his generosity.

Finally, I must acknowledge the administration, students and faculty, especially Marj Havlick, at Le Collège Évangélique de Libamba, where I taught from 1973 to1980. They kindly accepted me into their community, where I learned many more important lessons than any knowledge I imparted to my students. Many of the lessons I learned in Africa are reflected in this book.

Introduction

The story of Joseph and his brothers may be one of the best-known of the Bible stories. It is, however, intended as more than the tale of a handsome young man unjustly wronged by his brothers who nevertheless overcomes incredible odds to become the savior of his family. Though rarely referenced by name, the major presence in the story is God. The adventures of Joseph and his brothers, the sons of Jacob, are intended to give us very important information about the nature of God and his relationship with humanity. When God is considered, the story is truly awesome.

I use the metaphor of a "gateway" to explain the function of the story in our understanding of God. A gateway is an entrance that has a closure. It is the means by which you get from one area to another. I think of it as an archway in a wall. When the gate is closed, no one can pass. But when the gate is opened, the passageway leads into the new area.

The world of the twenty-first century has few closed gateways that function as true barriers. We can easily find the means to go around a blocked gate. But gateway has a secondary meaning. In our present internet age, a gateway is the device, or software, that connects two different networks. I am working at my computer. The computer is connected to a router that serves as a gateway to the internet. Without the router, my computer, on its own, cannot connect with the internet. I need the gateway to pass from one area, my computer, to another area, the vast expanses of the internet.

The Judeo-Christian faith community has long acknowledged that the biblical text authoritatively tells us about God. If we want to know what God is like, how he relates to humanity and how humanity can relate to him, we look to the biblical text. For millennia, believers have found the biblical text to be a trustworthy exposition of humanity's experience of God. It is a gateway between the infinite Supreme Being and the finite life of humanity.

The Bible contains many different sections that are called books, with each book having its own name. The story of Jacob's family is found in the last thirteen chapters of the book of Genesis, the first book of the Bible. Genesis is a carefully crafted introduction to God. It gives the reader a basic understanding of who God is and how he relates to humanity. The book is neither a full understanding, nor a complete exposition; rather, it is a gateway to the other books of Scripture. If the reader understands what Genesis tells us about God, then the reader gets pointed in the right direction as she reads further in the Bible.

Genesis starts with the story of creation and the stately language used shows the enormous care the writer took in telling this story. "In the beginning God created the heavens and the earth" (Gen 1:1). All of creation is described in relationship to its Creator but also in harmony with each part. There is light separated from the darkness (1:4); the sky is separated from the earth (1:6–7); and the waters are separated from the dry land (1: 9–10). What was formless takes shape.

Then the creation is filled. The dry land has vegetation (1:11–13); the sky has lights (1:14–19); the air has birds and the waters have fish (1:20–23); the land has every kind of living creation. (1:24–25). Finally, humankind is created (1:26–27). What was void has been filled. Order has been established; everything is in perfect harmony. There is no chaos in God's creation; there is a structure.

But this ideal world, while very beautiful and appealing, is not the world we know. Certainly, by the time a child enters kindergarten, she knows that there is much to fear in the world. There is no attempt by the writer of Genesis to hide this reality.

By chapter three of the book of Genesis, disorder enters the human condition. Adam and Eve are exiled from the Garden of Eden (Genesis 3). There then follows increasing human acts of disorder, leading God to destroy almost all of his creation by means of a flood (Gen. 6:5—8:19) Even the subsequent do-over starting with Noah (Gen. 8:21–22) did not lead to a return to the original state of perfect harmony. Disorder continued until God destroyed the human attempt to build its own abiding structure, the Tower of Babel (Gen. 11:1–9). After creation, the Bible's introductory book does not tell a story of comfort and joy.

The Genesis text then shifts in its emphasis. God speaks directly to one specific person, Abraham, who listens and with his family enters into a relationship with God (Gen. 12:1–4). God promises blessing to Abraham in the form of descendants and land, (Gen. 17:3–8) two essentials for life to continue. God keeps his promise of descendants, in spite of Abraham's failings and those of his son, Isaac, and those of his grandson, Jacob. The promise of land in Genesis remains a future hope.

The book of Genesis concludes with the text we will explore in this book— Genesis 37–50. Just as the creation story and stories of Israel's first ancestors are well-organized, so the story of Jacob's family, Joseph, and his brothers brings a very carefully structured conclusion to the Genesis narrative. The story is set out in thirteen chapters, an usually large amount of Scripture for one continuous narrative. The story's placement as a conclusion to Genesis, along with its length and the care with which it is told, reflect its importance in the Bible's opening book.

I think of the structure of the book of Genesis as an arched gateway. My image is a gateway built of stone. The story of Jacob's family is, in my opinion, the keystone to the book of Genesis. The creation stories are the foundation of the arch; the various events that follow are well-hewn stones that build up the sides of the arch. The reader then comes to the conclusion, and here the writer sets out his teaching on the meaning of what has transpired. It is this story of Jacob's family that holds the two sides of the arch together. It is the top most stone that bears the weight of the two sides. It allows the gateway to stand, points the reader in the right direction and gives the reader admission to the fuller revelation of God contained in the remaining books of Scripture.

A Lawyer's Approach

It is very hard for the adult reader to consider the story of Jacob's family unencumbered by others' ideas. I have known the story since my childhood, have heard many sermons on these verses, probably preached on this passage, and taught the story to a seventh grade Sunday school class. The relevance of any Bible passage and the effectiveness of any teacher is well tested in the crucible of the adolescent mind. Before starting this project, I had little new to say about Joseph.

My fresh start began when I undertook the study of biblical Hebrew after practicing law for over thirty years. Reading a text in Hebrew is a labor-intensive job for the beginning Hebrew student. The effort requires the student to focus on each word, jot, and tittle. I started out thinking these chapters in the book of Genesis made up the saga of Joseph, a story relating how a resourceful, young Hebrew man learned how to succeed in business. Then in the second verse, the writer explains "This is the story of the family of Jacob" (Gen 37:2a). It is not the saga of Joseph but rather the story of an entire family. The title puts the emphasis on the relationships that bind Jacob's sons into a family. When you have to re-think even the title of the text, you realize there is more to the story than the adventures of Joseph.

I came to this text asking the same questions I would ask of a legal text. I have two basic questions. First, how do I determine what is happening? I look for the answer to the question, who did what to whom? This requires a careful reading of the text so that all the facts are clear. Second, how do I determine why the reader is being told these facts? The writer of a legal text is always advancing a point of view, not merely setting out a narrative. Her perspective may not be succinctly stated but is apparent when the reader follows the writer's reasoning.

Lawyers spend a lot of time interpreting texts. Law school is a crash course in how to read. The law student reads a mountain of legal opinions, the written decision a judge issues in each case that comes before her. A good opinion begins by setting out the central point of contention between the two parties in the case. The issue before the court is stated as a question. For example: Is a drunken man responsible for the damage he caused when he shot up a bar, even though he reasonably believed at the time that the gun he was firing contained only blanks?

The written opinion then sets out the facts the judge considers dispositive and how previous decisions suggest the answer to this specific case's question. The more important point, for those not directly involved in the case, is to be found in the judge's reasoning, the explanation given in the opinion for the judge's conclusion. The judge not only wants to give an answer to the specific question raised, but also wants her explanation to convince posterity that this is the correct answer.

In order to understand the judge's reasoning, the law student has to follow the judge's argument step by step. It is crucial not to assume that one knows how the judge reaches her decision. Every word written was chosen by the judge in order to advance her argument. The law student must come to understand the significance of the words chosen. A missed conjunction "but" in the last sentence of a paragraph can change the whole direction of the argument. The judge chooses each word with a purpose, and it is the law student's job to read carefully until that purpose is clear.

This working out the structure of the judge's reasoning is called briefing a case. A good lawyer will be briefing cases her entire career. In the brief, the law student is forced to write down in outline form each step in the judge's argument. The judge's opinion can be criticized, but first the lawyer must set out the steps the judge took to reach her decision.

As I began working on the story of Jacob's family, I realized the writer of this story was making an argument, advancing a perspective concerning the Lord's relationship with humanity. If the reader follows the writer's argument, as the law student understands the structure of the judge's opinion, then the reader is in a position to draw relevant conclusions about the story's intent.

Moreover, this writer tells of events and makes his argument in a way that is consistent with many concepts of American law. The writer is not a lawyer, but he understands how lawyers think and perceive the world; he follows a structure of reasoned decision making.

To return again to law school, at the end of the judge's written opinion there is always a precise answer to the case's central question. This is the judge's specific ruling in the case. If the law student misses all the steps in the judge's reasoning, there is still a definite answer to the question posed at the beginning by the judge. The answer in the above example is yes, a man impaired by alcohol consumption is not immune from the consequences of his actions, even if those actions may have appeared somewhat unintended at the time.

The writer of the story of Jacob's family does render a verdict on the issue he has raised. Twice in the story, once in the approximate middle and then at the end of the story, Joseph makes a brief summary. To begin to understand his summary, however, the reader must have worked through all that has gone on before this point in the story. Joseph does not attempt to set out the full significance of the events related in his summary. For the writer, what is of paramount importance is what Lord does or causes to happen, not how Joseph describes these actions. The actions, which have been narrated, constitute the writer's reasoning.

Having looked at what happened in the story and why the writer set out these events in his chosen order, I also consider why the writer told his story in this manner. In the American judicial system, a case can either be submitted to a judge or the case is submitted to a jury, usually twelve citizens, who as a group hear the evidence and render a verdict. When a case is presented to a jury, there is a lot of talking. No written arguments are submitted to the jury; the presentation is entirely verbal. The jury must listen carefully to what is being said in order to understand the significance of the events being related.

As a consequence of needing to convince a jury based on spoken words only, the lawyer must adapt her presentation so that it can be easily followed by the listening jury. There is no opportunity for the jury to go back and re-read a point in the lawyer's argument that was not clear when first heard. The juror must grasp the lawyer's meaning when it is spoken.

An oral argument requires a strong structure. The listener needs to understand how the argument is advancing. A good lawyer knows her case needs to tell a story that the jury can easily follow. The lawyer needs to present the evidence in a narrative arc that follows a chronological order that first establishes the background and then moves to the events that occurred, presenting them in the order in which they occurred and then drawing conclusions based on what the events signify. It helps to repeat significant points frequently so that these points in the argument remain uppermost in the listener's mind.

For millennia, people listened to the story of Jacob's family being read aloud. The structure of the written story is intended to be followed by a congregation that only hears the passage read. The story is structured like the lawyer's oral argument.

At the end of the trial, after all the witnesses have spoken, the lawyer makes a closing argument to the jury. This is the lawyer's chance to tell the jury the significance of the evidence that has been presented. She leads the jury step by step through the evidence and draws conclusions about what weight should be given the different pieces of evidence. The lawyer is summarizing, telling her story in the hope that the jury will adopt her version of events. The closing argument always ends with the lawyer asking the jury to decide in her favor.

The story of Jacob's family is the summary statement for the book of Genesis, what I earlier referred to as the keystone of the gateway. It is the writer's attempt to explain his understanding of God, and how God interacts with humanity. In the story itself, Joseph makes a summary statement about the significance of the events that have been related. The reader is left the task of deciding the merits of the case. Does the story of Jacob's family ring true with our understanding of the human experience? The faith community for millennia has affirmed that it does.

Rules of the Road

What follows is my lawyer's brief of the story of Jacob's family. This is not a study of the plethora of commentaries on these Bible verses developed over the centuries. This is not a study of all that has gone before and then an attempt to present an original reading of the text. Nor do I address the very interesting issues that arise when one looks at the question of who wrote this story. I study the text as it is set out in the Leningrad Codex, the oldest complete Hebrew Bible text, with the assumption that someone or some group, whom I refer to collectively as "the writer," carefully thought through and wrote out the final form of this text. The following is my view, as an attorney with basic knowledge and experience in the American legal system, of how the text is structured and some of the concepts underlying the presentation of events.

I am a beginning Hebrew student. My facility with that language is on a par with the batting average of a journeyman baseball player in the minor leagues. I hit the ball about 25 to 30 percent of the time. In spite of my short comings, the language used in the Hebrew text must control any discussion of the writer's intent in the story of Jacob's family. I personally love the poetry of the Miles Coverdale translation, but it is the Leningrad Codex that controls. Translations point the reader in the right direction but the nuances are found only in Hebrew.

Many of the characters in the story have names that begin with the letter J: Jacob, Joseph, and Judah. Jacob is also known by the name *Israel.* I have tried to use the name Jacob, but occasionally the Hebrew text, which I am citing, uses the name Israel. The other possible J name is Jehovah, the name used for God in older English translations. Jehovah is the Latinization of the Tetragrammaton, the four Hebrew letters used to identify God's name in Hebrew text. This is the name God uses to self-identify. Out of respect, a Jewish reader never pronounces the Tetragrammaton, but substitutes the Hebrew word *Adonai* which means Lord. In the text, when there is a reference to the Lord, it is referring specifically to God's name.

I come from a background steeped in the Reformation and particularly the thinking of John Calvin. One of my bedrock convictions is that all members of the faith community should read the Bible and become familiar with its stories; not simply rely on someone else's commentary on the text. To that end, I have placed the relevant biblical passage in the text so that it is read before I begin my discussion. In my text you will see references, in parentheses, to the specific verses I am discussing. Read my text and make sure I have not gone astray in my comments by looking at specific references that catch your attention.

As a lawyer, I am well aware that there is always another side to a story. The American judicial system is adversarial, meaning each side has the chance to present her case. Here is my side. I look forward to hearing the other side of the case—from you and other readers.

Three Breaches

Chapter 1

Joseph Betrayed

Genesis 37:1–4

Jacob settled in the land where his father had lived as an
alien, the land of Canaan. [2]This is the story of the family
of Jacob.

Joseph, being seventeen years old, was shepherding
the flock with his brothers; he was a helper to the sons of
Bilhah and Zilpah, his father's wives; and Joseph brought
a bad report of them to their father. [3]Now Israel loved
Joseph more than any other of his children, because he
was the son of his old age; and he had made him a long
robe with sleeves. [4]But when his brothers saw that their
father loved him more than all his brothers, they hated
him, and could not speak peaceably to him.

The writer begins the story of Jacob's family, Genesis 37–50, by placing his narrative in a physical location. "Jacob *settled* in the land where his father had lived as an alien, the land of Canaan" (37:1, emphasis added). This statement gives us an important clue about Jacob's status. Jacob is settled in the land of Canaan where his father, Isaac, was merely an alien. Jacob has some recognized rights in the land that allow him to have an established home. Jacob does not own the land as he was promised by God at Luz

(Gen 35:12), but as the story begins, the well-being of Jacob's family is in place. The family has a secure place to live.

The writer refers to past events by calling to mind Jacob's father, Isaac, son of Abraham. God blessed Abraham, stating he would be the ancestor of a multitude of nations and have the land of Canaan for a perpetual holding (17:1–8).[1] This blessing passed from Abraham to his chosen son Isaac (22:16–18) who in turn passed the blessing to Jacob (28:3–4). The reader of the prior chapters of the book of Genesis knows that this family has received God's blessing in the past.

Having established a context, the writer then defines his subject: this is the story of Jacob's family (37:2). While this passage is popularly known as the story of Joseph and his brothers, the narrative's main thrust is not about Joseph; it is about Jacob's entire family. The events that are recounted affect the whole family and a resolution is only in place when it covers the whole family. Families exist because of relationships. The story examines those relationships.

Joseph, the hero of the story, is introduced in the latter half of the second verse. Most of the action in the story concerns Joseph as he makes his way in the world. In part, the story of Jacob's family is Joseph's coming of age story. The modern reader is familiar with this type of story. *Huckleberry Finn*, for example, tells of a boy's life in pre-Civil War Missouri. But *Huckleberry Finn* is more than the story of a virtuous boy facing an inhospitable world where the hero renounces "the devil and all his works, the vain pomp and glory of the world, with all covetous desires of the same, and the sinful desires of the flesh."[2] Huck in his very unconventional way does all those things, but Twain's bigger purpose is to tell about the realities and consequences of living in a society that tolerates slavery. Twain is advocating an abolitionist point of view.

1. Unless otherwise noted, the chapter and verse references are to the book of Genesis; thus, here Genesis chapter 17, verses one through eight.

2. *Book of Common Prayer*, "The Ministration of Holy Baptism," 1924 edition. *The Church Pension Fund*, page 277.

The story of Jacob's family tells of one family's encounter with God. It advances an understanding of God and his relationship with his creation. With the example of how the Lord dealt with Jacob's family, the reader gains an understanding of how the Lord intends to relate to all of humanity. The story of Jacob's family is a model for the family of humankind.

Our hero, Joseph, is seventeen years old (37:20). The birth of Joseph is recounted in Genesis 30:22–24. The name "Joseph" is from the Hebrew verb *yasaph*, meaning to add or increase.[3] Rachel, Joseph's mother explains the reference at Joseph's birth, "saying, 'May the Lord *add* to me another son'" (30:24, emphasis added). The writer will pun on this name in the first two chapters of the story.

Joseph's age is important. In general, age as given in the Scriptures is a very hard concept for the modern reader. For example, Isaac is reported to be 180 years old at his death (35:28). This is an incredible age for a man who years before his death was described as old and "his eyes were dim" (27:1). How could he live so long in that condition with limited understanding of sanitation or medicine? Perhaps the given age for Isaac is merely a way of expressing the idea of an advanced old age, not a precise statement of chronological age.

In an exception to this general observation, Joseph's age of seventeen should be understood as accurate. Modern readers will find this a very credible chronological age based on how Joseph acts and reacts to his family. Seventeen is usually a difficult time for young men. In modern literature, both Holden Caulfield in *Catcher in the Rye*, and Jim Stark in the movie *Rebel Without a Cause* are seventeen-year-olds. It is the season of rising sap; there is much ferment. The seventeen-year-old is fully grown and wants to seize what he perceives to be his rightful place in the family and society at large. He tests limits and seeks to establish his own personality free from the restraint of family obligations. This testing

3. All references to the Hebrew text come from the Westminster Leningrad Codex (see Tanach.us).

usually ends up with both the seventeen-year-old and the family taking some hard knocks and leaving bruises.

Moreover, while the young man may be fully grown, he is not fully mature in his decision making. He is often so self-involved with establishing his own personality that he fails to recognize the consequences his actions have on others. Being seventeen may have been on the mind of the psalmist when he prays, "Do not remember the sins of my youth" (Ps. 25:7a).

Joseph's actions in the first chapter of this story are consistent with our modern understanding of a seventeen-year-old. The ambiguity of Joseph's status in the family is reflected in the language used to describe him. Although not emphasized in the English translation, Joseph in verse 2 of the Hebrew text is called a *naar*, a young man, but later in verse 34, he is called a *yeled,* a boy or child. His brothers are ambiguous about his status.

At the beginning of the story, our hero is found tending the flock of sheep with his brothers (37:2). Jacob has twelve sons. The individual sons and their respective mothers are named in Genesis 35:23–26. Joseph is out with his half-brothers Dan, Naphtali, Gad and Asher, the sons of Bilhah and Zilpah.

The reference to Jacob's sons reminds the reader that Jacob has a large family. Moreover, it takes four men and a boy to shepherd the flock. It is the nature of sheep to wander. The number of shepherds suggests that this is a large flock because more than one man is required to keep the sheep in order. Jacob is well on the way to fulfilling God's blessing at Luz, "be fruitful and multiply; a nation and a company of nations shall come from you" (35:11). Jacob has become wealthy in the land of Canaan and is blessed with many sons.

These facts raise the question of who will inherit Jacob's wealth? Who will receive God's blessing? God chose Abraham, an individual, in the first generation. (12:1–3) God chose Isaac, Abraham's son in the second generation (17:19). Abraham had an older son, Ishmael, but he was not chosen (17:20–21). In the third generation, Jacob tricked Isaac into giving him the blessing in place of his older brother Esau (27:18–29). God confirmed this blessing on Jacob at Luz (35:11–12). So far in the book of Genesis, it is only one individual in each generation who is chosen by God. This story covers the fourth generation. While there is an expectation that the oldest will be given the blessing, (see the story of Jacob buying Esau's birthright, Genesis 25:29–34) the selection of both Isaac and Jacob show that God does not abide by the concept of primogenitor. Over this entire story hangs the questions: Who will God choose? What will become of Jacob's wealth? These questions are surely on the minds of Jacob's sons and will control their actions and reactions. The reader should also keep them in mind.

All is not well with Jacob's family. Jacob loves Joseph more than his other sons (v. 3). Joseph's brothers are very aware that Joseph is the favored one (v. 4). The family's problems start when Joseph brings a bad report to Jacob about the activities of his half-brothers. One assumes it did not go well for the brothers. At seventeen, the reader expects Joseph not to tattle on his older brothers. This report introduces a sub-theme in the story; the sons of Jacob get in trouble when they are away from home, in this case out tending sheep. Repeatedly, the writer relates that the brothers travel somewhere and get in trouble.

The brothers' irritation with Joseph is compounded by Jacob giving Joseph a special garment, a long robe with sleeves (v. 3). The description of this robe is based on ambiguous Hebrew language; it is not clear how this robe looked. Traditionally in English translations, the description is rendered as "a coat of many colors." This translation gives rise, with poetic license, to the title of the popular Lloyd-Weber musical, *Joseph and the Technicolor Dreamcoat*. For our purposes, the garment is special. It is tangible evidence for all to see that Joseph is preferred. It may also be a sign that Jacob will make Joseph the chosen one, his sole heir. This special treatment irritates the brothers to the level of hatred. The brothers are not able to speak peaceably, *shalom,* to Joseph (v. 4). The family's well-being appears broken.

This is the first strike against Joseph. He has acted badly when he tattles on his brothers. As a seventeen-year-old he should have known better, but he fails to meet expectations. The family endures these irritations because they are a necessary step toward adulthood. The seventeen-year-old makes mistakes, but in time learns to avoid repeating these errors in judgment. This latter situation occurs as an adolescent moves into adulthood. Getting there is a bumpy but necessary route.

The writer, however, gives us no indication that Joseph did anything to gain his father's favor. Jacob should have known better than to play favorites. Jacob's father, Isaac, preferred his brother Esau because Esau was a skillful hunter and Isaac was fond of game (25:28). Joseph has no special skill. Joseph is preferred because of his status as the son of Jacob's old age (v. 3), a status over which Joseph has no control.

> Genesis 37:5–11
>
> 5 Once Joseph had a dream, and when he told it to his
> brothers, they hated him even more. 6He said to them,
> 'Listen to this dream that I dreamed. 7There we were,
> binding sheaves in the field. Suddenly my sheaf rose and
> stood upright; then your sheaves gathered around it, and
> bowed down to my sheaf.' 8His brothers said to him, 'Are
> you indeed to reign over us? Are you indeed to have dominion over us?' So they hated him even more because
> of his dreams and his words.
>
> 9 He had another dream, and told it to his brothers,
> saying, 'Look, I have had another dream: the sun, the
> moon, and eleven stars were bowing down to me.' 10But
> when he told it to his father and to his brothers, his father
> rebuked him, and said to him, 'What kind of dream is
> this that you have had? Shall we indeed come, I and your
> mother and your brothers, and bow to the ground before
> you?' 11So his brothers were jealous of him, but his father
> kept the matter in mind.

The tension increases when Joseph tells his brothers about a dream he had. Before the dream is related, the writer tells us that Joseph's act of relating the dream causes the brothers' hatred to increase (v. 5). The verb for increase, or "added to," is *yasaph,* a word play on Joseph's name. This writer is not only an effective advocate but presents his case with artistry.

Joseph's dream has all the brothers in the field binding sheaves. Joseph's sheaf arises and the other sheaves bow down to it (v. 7). The brothers offer an interpretation: Joseph will have dominion over the family (v. 8).

The telling of the first dream concludes with the brothers hating Joseph even more (v. 8). The verb *yasaph*, to add or increase, is used again for the concept of even more. The brothers started out increasing their hate and conclude this episode increasing their hatred. The three-fold repetition of the same verb, "to hate," between verse 4 and verse 8 reinforces the importance of the brothers' reaction.

This episode introduces the theme of dream interpretation which will play an important part later in the story. At this point, the writer does not tell us the origins of this dream nor its import, he merely introduces the story's first dream. The brothers perceive that the dream comes from Joseph's self-aggrandizing view of himself as the chosen one of his generation. Moreover, the dream seems to be some indicator of the future. Both the verbs "to reign" *(malak),* and "have dominion" (*mashal),* are emphasized in Hebrew by repeating each verb twice. The verb "bow down" is repeated three times in verses 7 to 10, reinforcing that Joseph will have dominion over his brothers. The brothers' hatred arises from fear of Joseph's future power, which is emphasized in the dream.

Joseph then tells the entire family of a second dream. The sun, the moon and eleven stars, bow down to Joseph (v. 9). This time Jacob offers an interpretation that seems to be a hypothesis since it is stated in the form of a question; will Joseph have dominion not only over his brothers but also over his father and mother?[4]

The brothers' reaction is further specified. They are jealous. Jacob's reaction is more muted. On hearing the dream, Jacob rebukes Joseph (v. 10). Throughout this story, Jacob is indisputably the one who rules over his family. Everyone defers to Jacob. Jacob has clear dominion over his large family. He may well be

4. There is a problem with the reference to Jacob's wife, Rachel, mother of Joseph. Her death is reported in an earlier text, 35:19. How can this dream be fulfilled when the person referenced has already died?

displeased with the idea that during his lifetime one of his sons will have dominion over the family.

Jacob, however, also has experience with dreams. God appeared to Jacob in a dream at Bethel/Luz (28:12–15). In that dream, the Lord spoke directly to Jacob and told him what the Lord intended to do on his behalf. Joseph's dreams are different. His dreams describe future events. There is no a direct revelation of the divine will where the Lord speaks to the dreamer. At this point, it is neither evident where Joseph's dreams come from nor their power. Because Jacob has experience with dreams, he does not dismiss Joseph's dreams as meaningless, but merely keeps the matter in mind. The reader should also have them in mind for future reference.

The well-being of Jacob's family is broken. For the brothers, there are three strikes against Joseph: first, he tattles and then he tells two dreams in which the brothers bow down to him. Three is an important number for the writer. The whole presentation of the story is built around the number three; each section has three parts, events are presented in groups of three, and there are three outcomes that arise from a deed. Any argument is easier to follow when there is a clear structure; the path of the argument should be clearly set out, not a meandering track. With this three-point structure established, when the listener hears of two events, one can anticipate a third. For example, if the congregation hears at a wedding the words: "love, honor . . ." everyone knows that there is a third verb in the charge and what it is. The entire congregation may not agree with the charge, but the structure is known. The presentation of the third element completes the concept for the listener and the listener's attention does not wander off in search of the third element.

Genesis 37:12–28

> 12 Now his brothers went to pasture their father's flock
> near Shechem. 13And Israel said to Joseph, 'Are not your
> brothers pasturing the flock at Shechem? Come, I will
> send you to them.' He answered, 'Here I am.' 14So he said
> to him, 'Go now, see if it is well with your brothers and

with the flock; and bring word back to me.' So he sent
him from the valley of Hebron.

He came to Shechem, [15]and a man found him wandering in the fields; the man asked him, 'What are you
seeking?' [16]'I am seeking my brothers,' he said; 'tell me,
please, where they are pasturing the flock.' [17]The man
said, 'They have gone away, for I heard them say, "Let
us go to Dothan."' So Joseph went after his brothers, and
found them at Dothan. [18]They saw him from a distance,
and before he came near to them, they conspired to
kill him. [19]They said to one another, 'Here comes this
dreamer. [20]Come now, let us kill him and throw him into
one of the pits; then we shall say that a wild animal has
devoured him, and we shall see what will become of his
dreams.' [21]But when Reuben heard it, he delivered him
out of their hands, saying, 'Let us not take his life.' [22]Reu-
ben said to them, 'Shed no blood; throw him into this pit
here in the wilderness, but lay no hand on him'—that he
might rescue him out of their hand and restore him to
his father. [23]So when Joseph came to his brothers, they
stripped him of his robe, the long robe with sleeves that
he wore; [24]and they took him and threw him into a pit.
The pit was empty; there was no water in it.

[25] Then they sat down to eat; and looking up they saw
a caravan of Ishmaelites coming from Gilead, with their
camels carrying gum, balm, and resin, on their way to
carry it down to Egypt. [26]Then Judah said to his brothers,
'What profit is there if we kill our brother and conceal
his blood? [27]Come, let us sell him to the Ishmaelites, and
not lay our hands on him, for he is our brother, our own
flesh.' And his brothers agreed. [28]When some Midianite
traders passed by, they drew Joseph up, lifting him out of
the pit, and sold him to the Ishmaelites for twenty pieces
of silver. And they took Joseph to Egypt.

In verse 12, the narrative turns to action. So far, the family has been talking and reacting to Joseph. In this section, the writer uses action verbs: went, come, send, go, see, and bring. In verse 14, there are three imperatives. The time of talking is over. The family is on the move.

Ten of Jacob's sons take the flock to Shechem (v. 12). This location is some distance away from home. Jacob has no news of either his sons or his flock (v. 14). Jacob dispatches Joseph to see how things are going and to report back (v. 14).

Jacob appears oblivious to his sons' hatred of Joseph. Yet, the reader knows that the brothers are not on good terms with Joseph; they do not speak peaceably to him (v. 4). Jacob surely heard these words. It is a high risk move to send his most beloved son by himself, far away and into the hands of his jealous brothers.

Joseph, the obedient son, goes (v. 13). He arrives at his destination, Shechem, and finds the brothers have moved on. A stranger sees Joseph wandering in the fields of Shechem (v. 15). The danger inherent in sending the boy alone becomes real. Joseph is by himself and confronted by a stranger. Is this man friend or foe? Being alone and seventeen, the physical advantage in the confrontation is with the stranger.

Joseph asks about the whereabouts of his brothers and having received the answer, he pursues his family to Dothan, which is even further away (vv. 15–17). Joseph misperceives the situation. He fails to understand his brothers' hatred against him. This is understandable since he is seventeen years old and concerned with his own perceptions of the world, not how others perceive him.

Joseph relies on the loyalty of his family, but this reliance is misplaced. Family loyalty is a bedrock condition for survival in the land of Canaan. One cannot survive for long on one's own in the desert. Fortunately, at Shechem Joseph met a friend. What occurs next, happens because Joseph is alone. The family does not protect him.

Alone, Joseph is subject to extreme violence. This is what Cain, who killed his brother Abel out of jealousy, realized when the Lord announced his punishment, 'You [Cain] will be a fugitive and a wanderer on the earth' (4:12). Cain responded, 'My punishment is greater than I can bear! . . . I shall be a fugitive and a wanderer on the earth, and anyone who meets me may kill me' (vv. 13–14). The Lord then cushions the blow to Cain by providing some protection while Cain is without family (v. 15). Family loyalty and the ability of family members to trust each other is a fundamental requirement for survival. It allows the family to work together and defend itself from outsiders. Left alone without family relationships, one's chances of survival in Canaan are slim.

As Joseph approaches Dothan, his brothers see him and plot to cause his death (v. 18). Far from home, the brothers decide to take matters into their own hands. They are jealous. They perceive, wrongly, that Joseph is a threat. They believe Joseph will be the chosen one and inherit all of Jacob's wealth. When they see him approaching, they decide to kill him.

American law would characterize the brothers' action as "self-help." This occurs when a private party decides to correct a wrong on her own without the sanction of the court. An example would be a creditor repossessing a car after the owner failed to pay the outstanding car loan. The wrong in this example is the failure to pay on the loan. The self-help is the creditor acting to correct the wrong by taking possession of the car. The courts tolerate this self-help because a car is very mobile, and there is a high risk the debtor will flee with the car before the creditor can seek court sanctioned action. The problem is that the creditor acts on his perception of the situation; the creditor believes he knows the truth of the matter. There is no opportunity for the debtor to correct any misperception by the creditor. The courts dislike self-help. The courts prefer an established procedure where all concerned can test the truth of the matter.

These same problems exist when the sons of Jacob pursue a course of self-help. Their goal is to correct what they perceive is a wrong, to cut off Joseph's future domination: 'We shall see what will become of his dreams' (v. 20). This is a rhetorical question, reflecting derision, and anticipates a negative answer. The brothers act based on the misperception that Joseph is a threat to their independence and their hope to inherit from their father.

At home, the brothers' hatred intensified over time. At Dothan, the brothers' rage diminishes as Joseph comes into their presence. The diminishment comes in three stages. The brothers' first plan is to kill him outright and throw his body into a pit (v.

20). Reuben tempers that plan by suggesting they simply throw Joseph into a pit. This option leaves open the possibility that Joseph will rescued (v. 22).

Reuben's injunction "Shed no blood . . ." (v. 22) is important. The reader is reminded of the earlier story of Cain and Abel (4:1–16). When Cain kills Abel, and then prevaricates when confronted by the Lord, the Lord responds 'Listen; your brother's blood is crying out to me from the ground!' (4:10). As the brothers plot Joseph's death, the reader has a good idea how this story should end. If Joseph dies in the pit, and if there is consistency in God's judgment, then the brothers should be punished as Cain was.

The brothers act on Reuben's proposal. Three things happen to Joseph. First, Joseph is stripped of his special robe (37:23). Joseph is naked in the desert. Then his brothers throw him in a pit (v. 24), which Reuben has described as "here in the wilderness" (v. 22), foreclosing any help of assistance from passersby. Finally, the writer adds to the tension by stating "The pit was empty; there was no water in it" (v. 24). The empty pit is a very telling detail. No one can survive for long without water in the desert. The writer confirms that Joseph is in a dry pit, not an unused well. Joseph's situation is dire. He is naked, in a pit, in the wilderness, without water. Death is imminent.

Judah, however, makes a third proposal that further ameliorates Joseph's situation. He recalls to his brothers their duty not to kill Joseph. ". . . He is our brother, our own flesh" (v. 27). Judah understands the principle that the family must stand together to protect each other, the family has a duty of loyalty to each other. But Judah's understanding of the family's duty of loyalty is too narrow. According to Judah, the duty only extends to not killing Joseph. This is the same reasoning Cain used when he asked the question, "Am I my brother's keeper?" (4:9). The answer to Cain's question is yes, you are your brother's keeper. Judah's interpretation is also wrong. This duty of family loyalty requires more than preventing your younger brother from being slaughtered.

Judah seeks to side step his duty of loyalty by transforming the encounter with Joseph into a commercial transaction. Again, three things happen to Joseph. The naked seventeen-year-old is drawn up from the bottom of the pit, he is lifted out of the pit, and he is sold to a passing caravan of Ishmaelites for twenty pieces of silver. They take him to Egypt (v. 28).

> Genesis 37:29–36
>
> 29 When Reuben returned to the pit and saw that Joseph
> was not in the pit, he tore his clothes. 30 He returned to
> his brothers, and said, 'The boy is gone; and I, where
> can I turn?' 31 Then they took Joseph's robe, slaughtered
> a goat, and dipped the robe in the blood. 32 They had the
> long robe with sleeves taken to their father, and they said,
> 'This we have found; see now whether it is your son's
> robe or not.' 33 He recognized it, and said, 'It is my son's
> robe! A wild animal has devoured him; Joseph is without
> doubt torn to pieces.' 34 Then Jacob tore his garments, and
> put sackcloth on his loins, and mourned for his son for
> many days. 35 All his sons and all his daughters sought to
> comfort him; but he refused to be comforted, and said,
> 'No, I shall go down to Sheol to my son, mourning.' Thus
> his father bewailed him. 36 Meanwhile the Midianites had
> sold him in Egypt to Potiphar, one of Pharaoh's officials,
> the captain of the guard.

The consequences set in quickly; these come in three stages. The brothers originally intended to slaughter Joseph by their own hands and then to say that Joseph was devoured by a wild animal (37:20), a very plausible scenario since Joseph was traveling alone. This explanation is improved after the sale of Joseph into slavery. The brothers slaughter a goat and dip Joseph's special coat in its blood (v. 31).

Second, they take the physical evidence, the bloody robe, to Jacob. The brothers give no explanation concerning the significance of the robe. Jacob draws the conclusion that Joseph has been torn to pieces (v. 33). The physical evidence the brothers present is intended to mislead Jacob and bolster the lie that Joseph was devoured by a wild animal.

Finally, Jacob's grief is inconsolable. He declares, "'No, I shall go down to Sheol to my son, mourning'" (v. 35). The well-being of

Jacob's family is shattered by the brothers' jealousy. Jacob suggests he will go down to Sheol, the place of the dead; often compared to being in a pit. The Psalmist writes:

> For my soul is full of troubles,
> and my life draws near to Sheol.
> I am counted among those who go down to the Pit;
> down to the Pit;
> I am like those who have no help,
> like those forsaken among the dead,
> like the slain that lie in a grave,
> like those whom you remember no more,
> for they are cut off from your hand.
> You have put me in the depths of the Pit,
> in the regions dark and deep.
> Your wrath lies heavy upon me,
> and you overwhelm me with your waves. (Ps. 88:3–7)

There will be no peace for Jacob. He foresees that his life will be a pit of despair. Joseph is literally out of the pit, but sold as a slave to Potiphar in Egypt (v. 36), a seemingly hopeless situation.

In this opening chapter, the writer has established a pattern for his presentation of events. Things happen in groups of three. The structural pattern of chapter 37, will also control the presentation of evidence in chapters 38 and 39. In these chapters, after establishing the context of the passage, the writer sets out a problem, specifically a person perceives that he is aggrieved because of another. The injured person seeks to solve the problem by taking action, pursuing a remedy of self-help. Finally, there are consequences to the action taken.

In chapter 37, the writer also presents his understanding of wrong doing. Wrong doing is the major theme for the first three chapters of the story. The writer's description in chapter 37 of wrong doing becomes a model for how he describes the injuries incurred in the next two chapters. The narrative assumes an obligation, or duty of loyalty, on the part of family members. It is the duty of the older brothers to watch over Joseph, to protect him; not to cause him harm. The brothers commit a consequential wrong when they fail to do their duty. Because of this omission, Joseph suffers serious harm. His life is taken away from him and he becomes the property of another (v. 36). This pattern will be repeated in the next two chapters.

This analysis of a problem is familiar to the American lawyer. The actions described would today be considered a tort, or civil wrong. For a tort to occur, the law must find that one party owes a duty to another. For example, a driver has a duty to other motorists to drive in a safe manner and to respect the laws of the road. The facts then need to show that the duty was breached. A common occurrence would be a driver running a stop sign, hitting another vehicle. The breach, the failure to obey the stop sign, causes a collision. Finally, to have a tort, the facts must show that the breach of duty, failure to obey the laws of the road, caused damage to the other party, the woman whose car was hit suffers injury. These four elements: duty, breach, causation, and damages make up the American concept of tort.

The concept of a tort grew out of the common law, a series of individual judicial decisions recorded in English courts over hundreds of years. Oliver Wendell Holmes, Jr. famously wrote in his book *The Common Law*, "The life of the law has not been logic; it has been experience."[5] Experience, according to Holmes, arises from ". . . the customs, belief or needs . . ."[6] of the community. A problem arises and the court fashions a remedy which is implemented to solve the difficulty. "The substance of the law at any given time pretty nearly corresponds, so far as it goes, with what is then understood to be convenient . . . ."[7]

In order to be efficient and to offer predictability, the rule arose that when a similar problem comes before a court, the judge looks to past decisions to determine what the answer should be.

5. O. W. Holmes, Jr., *The Common Law* (1881); citing the 32nd printing (Boston: Little, Brown and Company, 1938), 1.

6. Ibid., 5.

7. Ibid., 1–2.

As the decisions multiply, a student can look back at the specific rulings and begin to see a possible paradigm that gives some structure to the rationale for the decisions.[8]

Holmes begins his discussion in *The Common Law* with the problem of vengeance. Someone in the community injures another. The basic human response is to want revenge. To prevent mayhem, judges fashioned rules about how vengeance was to be implemented and eventually offered compensation to the victim, rather than allow blood vengeance. The decisions continued until looking back legal scholars developed the concepts of tort.[9]

The writer of the Jacob story is developing an argument in this tradition. He tells about a problem in the community. What happens when the people of God go astray? The brothers owe a duty of care to Joseph. They breach that duty when they allow him to be carried off to Egypt. This failure to act causes Joseph injury. He suffers damages; his freedom is taken away. Chapters 38 and 39 tell about other wrong doing in the community.

The writer then moves forward in the next chapters, setting out solutions or remedies to the problems described in the first chapters, thus answering the question how the people of God will continue to receive the Lord's blessing which sustains their lives when things go wrong. The writer's reasoning and presentation of evidence concerning the problem facing his community is consistent with the reasoning that millennia later would give rise to the concept of a civil wrong. The writer is in the position of Holmes' common law judge, but the writer's scope is much greater.

8. This entire discussion of Justice Holmes' famous quote is based on the research and arguments found in Brian Hawkins, "The Life of the Law: What Holmes Meant," 33 Wittier Law Review 323 (2012); available at SSRN: http// ssrn.com/abstract=1753389.

9. Holmes, *The Common Law*, chapter 1.

Chapter 2

Tamar Betrayed

Genesis 38:1–5

It happened at that time that Judah went down from his
brothers and settled near a certain Adullamite whose
name was Hirah. [2]There Judah saw the daughter of a
certain Canaanite whose name was Shua; he married her
and went in to her. [3]She conceived and bore a son; and
he named him Er. [4]Again she conceived and bore a son
whom she named Onan. [5]Yet again she bore a son, and
she named him Shelah. She was in Chezib when she bore
him.

In chapter 38, the writer shifts the focus of his narrative to the story of Judah, a son of Jacob. Following the pattern evident in the previous chapter, this chapter is built around a three-point structure. After establishing a context, the writer sets out a problem. The characters in the narrative then act to solve the problem. Finally, there are consequences to the solution chosen.

One of the main characters in this chapter is Judah, Joseph's older brother. The fact that the story is centered on a later time in Judah's life, after Joseph's disappearance, makes it clear that the sons of Jacob will not be punished as Cain was (Gen. 4:11–16). The story of Cain and Abel establish the precedent that fratricide results in exile. With this present narrative, it becomes apparent that some other remedy for the wrong doing of the brothers will be found. God is not bound by the rule of *stare decisis*, a concept in American law which holds that a judge should follow precedent and reach the same decision as previous judges when the facts of the case are similar.

This chapter telling of Judah and his daughter-in-law Tamar is a surprise. In all the other chapters of the story, Joseph is the hero. The writer, however, has clearly indicated that the story concerns Jacob's family, not only Joseph. By addressing another family member, the writer broadens the story's perspective to include the whole family.

The writer starts this new episode by telling the location of the action. Judah has left his brothers and has gone to live near a man named Hirah (38:1) The reader should be alert for trouble. Judah is far from home. Judah makes his way in the world. He marries a woman who is never named, but referred to simply as the daughter of Shua. She bears him three sons: Er, Onan, and Shelah (vv. 2–5). Describing the third son's birth, the passage says Judah's wife "yet again she bore a son [Shelah]" (v. 5). The Hebrew text uses the verb *yasaph,* translated as "yet again," to describe the additional birth. This is another word play in Hebrew on the name of Joseph.

> Genesis 38:6–11
>
> [6]Judah took a wife for Er his firstborn; her name was Tamar. [7]But Er, Judah's firstborn, was wicked in the sight of the Lord, and the Lord put him to death. [8]Then Judah said to Onan, 'Go in to your brother's wife and perform the duty of a brother-in-law to her; raise up offspring for your brother.' [9]But since Onan knew that the offspring would not be his, he spilled his semen on the ground whenever he went in to his brother's wife, so that he would not give offspring to his brother. [10]What he did was displeasing in the sight of the Lord, and he put him to death also. [11]Then Judah said to his daughter-in-law Tamar, 'Remain a widow in your father's house until my son Shelah grows up'—for he feared that he too would die, like his brothers. So Tamar went to live in her father's house.

Judah's family lives at Chezib. Life moves forward and eventually Judah chooses a wife for his oldest son Er. The woman's name is Tamar (v. 6). With this marriage, the chapter's central problem arises. "Er, Judah's firstborn, was wicked in the sight of the Lord, and the Lord put him to death" (v. 7). No reason is given for the Lord's decision.

The death of Er gives rise to an obligation on the part of Judah's remaining sons, Onan and Shelah. "Then Judah said to Onan [the second son], 'Go in to your brother's wife and perform the duty of a brother-in-law to her; raise up offspring for your brother' (v. 8). The obligation to Tamar, Er's wife and Judah's daughter-in-law, is in effect though she is a non-Hebrew.

The obligation is very straight forward; "go in to Tamar," a Hebrew expression for sexual intercourse. The resulting child will be considered Er's child. Onan refuses to do his duty, manipulating the situation so that Tamar cannot become pregnant (v. 9). This is another misdirected attempt at self-help. Onan has a sure grasp of the truth. He understands his duty, but consciously acts to do wrong. Onan has breached his duty causing damage to Tamar. The elements of a tort are in place.

The Lord chooses to punish Onan. "What he did was displeasing in the sight of the Lord, and he put him [Onan] to death also" (v. 10). Death is not a remedy that allows the parties to go forward; it is by its nature a solution with no future. It is the end of hope. It should be recalled that Cain was not put to death when he killed Abel, but was given some protection for his life as a fugitive and wanderer (Gen. 4:15). In the story of Jacob's family, the Lord seeks to preserve the future of his chosen people and finds other remedies besides death to correct the wrongs committed. The deaths of Er and Onan are a narrow exception.

Judah also pursues a course of self-help. He sends Tamar away to her father's house because he fears Tamar is the cause of his sons' deaths (v. 11). The reader knows that the deaths were the Lord's doing (v 10), and that Judah is acting on a misperception. Judah justifies this exile by saying Tamar must wait until the third son grows up (v. 11). Both Judah and Onan's attempts at self-help are misdirected, since they are inconsistent with the Lord's will.

> Genesis 38:12–19
>
> 12 In course of time the wife of Judah, Shua's daughter, died; when Judah's time of mourning was over, he went up to Timnah to his sheep-shearers, he and his friend Hirah the Adullamite. [13]When Tamar was told, 'Your father-in-law is going up to Timnah to shear his sheep', [14]she put off her widow's garments, put on a veil, wrapped herself up, and sat down at the entrance to Enaim, which is on the road to Timnah. She saw that Shelah was grown up, yet she had not been given to him in marriage. [15]When Judah saw her, he thought her to be a prostitute, for she had covered her face. [16]He went over to her at the roadside, and said, 'Come, let me come in to you', for he did not know that she was his daughter-in-law. She said, 'What will you give me, that you may come in to me?' [17]He answered, 'I will send you a kid from the flock.' And she said, 'Only if you give me a pledge, until you send it.' [18]He said, 'What pledge shall I give you?' She replied, 'Your signet and your cord, and the staff that is in your hand.' So he gave them to her, and went in to her, and she conceived by him. [19]Then she got up and went away, and taking off her veil she put on the garments of her widowhood.

The narrative advances. Judah's wife dies, he mourns her for the required time, and then he goes with his friend from his home in Chezib to Timnah in order "to shear his sheep" (v. 13). Judah is away from home and Tamar hears of it. Tamar understands the truth of the situation. "She saw that Shelah [the third son] was grown up, yet she had not been given to him in marriage" (v. 14). Judah intends to make the wrong against Tamar permanent. He creates a hopeless situation for Tamar, since she has no recognizable path to conceive a child, her right under the law.

Tamar takes three actions to remedy her situation. She takes off her widow clothes, she wraps herself in a veil, and she sits down "at the entrance to Enaim, which is on the road to Timnah" (v.

14). Tamar is pursuing a course of self-help that requires her to disguise herself. She is acting based on a true understanding of the facts. The story will reveal whether her actions are in keeping with the Lord's will.

Judah continues to act on his misperceptions. As he travels to the sheep shearing, he sees Tamar but takes the woman sitting at the entrance to Enaim to be a prostitute (v. 15). Tamar's disguise is effective. Judah, apparently suffering from gonzo sexual desire, enters into negotiations with the prostitute. Away from home, Judah goes astray. Judah again pursues an improper commercial transaction. In the earlier case, he illicitly sold his brother to a passing caravan (37:27). In this case he seeks to buy illicit services from a sex worker. The illegality of the arrangement with the sex worker is later confirmed by the judgment on the prostitute (37:24).

In the dialogue between Judah and Tamar, the writer shows a very sophisticated understanding of contract law. For an enforceable contract to exist in American law, there must be an offer, an acceptance of the offer, and something of value to each party exchanged—what the law calls *consideration*. Often this is money given in exchange for a product or service.

All three elements exist in this dialogue. Judah makes the offer: 'Come, let me come in to you' (v. 16). Tamar does not immediately accept. This is an arms-length transaction, meaning each party is free to walk away from the negotiations. This is not a sexual assault. Judah is offering to buy services. And even though the services are illicit, Judah is honorably pursuing contract negotiations.

Tamar seeks to define the terms of the consideration. Judah has not said what, if anything, he will pay. She responds directly to his offer, 'What will you give me, that you may come in to me?' (v. 16). The subject matter of the contract is clearly defined: sexual services from Tamar. At this point, the consideration remains to be negotiated.

Judah refines his offer by saying he will give a kid from his flock—something of value—for the services (v. 17). Tamar is shrewd in her response. It is apparent that the kid is at Timnah with the other sheep. Judah is asking for services in consideration for a promised future payment. That is always a very delicate situation in commercial transactions. In the barter system, payment is made and then the services are rendered. It is the experience of humankind that once services are rendered, the recipient has a strong tendency to forget to fulfill his side of the bargain.

The well-established protocol for this situation is for the service provider to hold something of value from the recipient until the full consideration for the contract is paid. Tamar continues to show that she is the more sophisticated negotiator. She asks for a pledge, a deposit, something of value that she will hold until the debt is paid (v. 17). If the recipient were to default on the contract, she would have proof of the contract and the right to pursue the deadbeat in court. She is asking for tangible evidence of the contract's existence. This is of extreme importance when the parties make an oral contract, where the terms of the contract are not written. With the pledges in hand, Tamar would have a cognizable claim against Judah if he were to fail to deliver the promised consideration, a kid sheep.

Judah appears dumbfounded that a sex worker would question his promise and require legally enforceable evidence of the contract. He asks, 'What pledge shall I give you?' (v. 18). Tamar has a ready answer: she asks for three things from Judah—his signet, his cord, and his staff (v. 18). Just one piece of evidence can be misconstrued, just as was the case when Joseph's bloody robe was presented to Jacob, and he imagined incorrectly that Joseph was dead. But obtaining a second piece of evidence makes a very strong case, and a third piece of evidence becomes overwhelming. Tamar is right to ask for three pledges, thus making her evidence iron clad.

The contract negotiations are over. The terms have been freely agreed to by both parties. The offer is for sexual services from Tamar. The consideration is future payment of a lamb by Judah; three items are given as security for the future payment. Judah shows his acceptance by handing over the specified items. Tamar accepts by allowing Judah to go in to her (v. 18). The self-help is effective. Tamar conceives (v. 18).

The passage ends with Tamar taking three actions. They are in reverse order of the three actions she took at the beginning. She stands up, she takes off her veil, and she puts on her widow garments (v. 19). From the observable facts, she appears to be in the same position as she was at the beginning of this episode, but everything is different.

Genesis 38:20–30

[20] When Judah sent the kid by his friend the Adullamite,
to recover the pledge from the woman, he could not find
her. [21]He asked the townspeople, 'Where is the temple
prostitute who was at Enaim by the wayside?' But they
said, 'No prostitute has been here.' [22]So he returned to
Judah, and said, 'I have not found her; moreover, the
townspeople said, "No prostitute has been here."' [23]Judah
replied, 'Let her keep the things as her own, otherwise we
will be laughed at; you see, I sent this kid, and you could
not find her.'

[24] About three months later Judah was told, 'Your
daughter-in-law Tamar has played the whore; moreover
she is pregnant as a result of whoredom.' And Judah said,
'Bring her out, and let her be burned.' [25]As she was being brought out, she sent word to her father-in-law, 'It
was the owner of these who made me pregnant.' And she
said, 'Take note, please, whose these are, the signet and
the cord and the staff.' [26]Then Judah acknowledged them
and said, 'She is more in the right than I, since I did not
give her to my son Shelah.' And he did not lie with her
again.

[27] When the time of her delivery came, there were
twins in her womb. [28]While she was in labour, one put
out a hand; and the midwife took and bound on his
hand a crimson thread, saying, 'This one came out first.'
[29]But just then he drew back his hand, and out came his
brother; and she said, 'What a breach you have made for
yourself!' Therefore he was named Perez. [30]Afterwards
his brother came out with the crimson thread on his
hand; and he was named Zerah.

There are three consequences to Tamar's self-help. First, Judah acts to fulfill his side of the bargain; he sends the promised consideration by his friend who is instructed to redeem the three pledged items and thus ending the prostitute's claim against Judah (v. 20). The friend cannot find the prostitute. Moreover, the townspeople report, "'No prostitute has been here'" (v. 21). The friend reports this fact to Judah (v. 22).

Judah fails to understand this testimony. Even though he has been given a critical piece of evidence, Judah has misperceived the situation. Judah remains locked in his perception that he had made a deal with a prostitute. He cavalierly dismisses the testimony of his friend, fearing that because he has not redeemed his pledges ". . . we will be laughed at" (v. 23). He may fear that the townspeople will not properly appreciate the overwhelming urgency of his sexual desire when he was walking down the road. The fear of how others may perceive him prevents Judah from understanding the truth of his situation.

The second consequence is that the truth begins to reveal itself three months later (v. 24). Again the writer gives a specific time period that reflects our modern understanding of human development. Tamar's pregnancy is beginning to show, what today is often called a "baby bump." This is reported to Judah. The witness states a conclusion grounded in a partial understanding of the truth. "Tamar has played the whore" (v. 24). Based on this half-truth, Judah condemns Tamar to be burned (v. 24).

The whole truth is then revealed to Judah. Tamar sends the three pledged items to Judah. She does not provide any further evidence. While the presentation of Joseph's one bloody garment led Jacob to the wrong conclusion; here the recognition of the three pledged items leads Judah to acknowledge the whole truth.

Judah recognizes that he is the father of the child. He breached his duty to Tamar because he "did not give her to my son Shelah" (v. 26). Judah honestly concludes, "She [Tamar] is more in the right than I" (v. 26).

The remedy Judah offers Tamar for the wrong he has committed is to have her restored to her former position in his family.

She is re-admitted as a member of his household. Later in the story (46:11) Tamar's sons are listed as members of Judah's family. Tamar is accepted as Judah's wife. The faulty judgment is vacated. The truth has prevailed.

Restoration is not the preferred remedy of the courts. It has too many problems to be an effective solution. The courts prefer money damages. The suffering caused by the wrong is not washed away; but with the payment of money, the wronged party and the offender are both able to move forward with their lives. The payment does not cure the wrong, but it provides the means for a future.

With restoration, the parties remain in a relationship. There can be numerous factors that cause problems in a relationship. Some are expressed and some unexpressed. Human relationships are too complex for the law to regulate effectively. The courts do not like the restoration of the parties in a dispute. Instead, they impose money damages that are easily defined. This remedy avoids the possibility of endless problems if the relationship is restored.

There may well have been numerous reasons Judah did not want Tamar to continue in his household. Judah's antipathy for Tamar may have been growing over the years. The death of his sons likely triggered his pain and Tamar's hopeless exile. One could conjecture from their commercial transaction that Tamar was more astute than Judah. Over time Judah may have come to realize this and did not like having someone that smart in his household.

The writer points out the limitations of Tamar's restoration. She is accepted into the household, but Judah "did not lie with her again" (v. 26). Tamar is not fully restored as a wife. Judah neither forgives nor forgets Tamar's clever ploy of self-help.

The Hebrew text again gives a word play on Joseph's name, using the verb *yasaph* to indicate that Judah did not add to his carnal knowledge of her. This gets translated, "he did not lie with her again" (v. 26). By this reference Joseph is slyly recalled to the reader's attention.

The third consequence of Judah's contract with Tamar is the birth of twin boys, Perez and Zerah. The birth is complicated. Zerah is the first to appear, but Perez is the first to be born (vv. 28–30). Perez's name has particular importance. The name comes from the Hebrew verb *parats*, meaning to break out, or burst forth. The word is used three times in one Hebrew sentence (v. 29). Literally, Tamar's womb was torn as her twins seek to be born. The triple repetition indicates the importance of the word.

The NRSV uses the word "breach" to describe Perez tearing Tamar's womb. The term breach is also used in American law to indicate when a party fails to perform a duty. With a tort, the person who fails to do his duty has caused a breach in the fabric of society just as Tamar's flesh was breached by the birth of Perez. Onan breached his duty to Tamar. Joseph's brothers breached their duty to Joseph.

Chapter 38 proposes a possible way to sew up the torn social fabric—the restoration of the parties. There is no remedy proposed for the breach caused by the sale of Joseph. That situation appears hopeless.

Looking forward, chapter 38 provides the structural model for the entire story of Jacob's family. The first three chapters of the story describe three breaches, or wrongdoings. The second section covers three restorations that rectify the wrongdoing, and the third section addresses three consequences or deaths that conclude the narrative arc.

Chapter 3

Joseph Betrayed Again

Genesis 39:1–6

Now Joseph was taken down to Egypt, and Potiphar, an
officer of Pharaoh, the captain of the guard, an Egyptian,
bought him from the Ishmaelites who had brought him
down there. [2]The LORD was with Joseph, and he became
a successful man; he was in the house of his Egyptian
master. [3]His master saw that the LORD was with him,
and that the LORD caused all that he did to prosper in
his hands. [4]So Joseph found favour in his sight and at-
tended him; he made him overseer of his house and put
him in charge of all that he had. [5]From the time that he
made him overseer in his house and over all that he had,
the LORD blessed the Egyptian's house for Joseph's sake;
the blessing of the LORD was on all that he had, in house
and field. [6]So he left all that he had in Joseph's charge;
and, with him there, he had no concern for anything
but the food that he ate. Now Joseph was handsome and
good-looking.

THE WRITER'S FOCUS IN chapter 39 returns to Joseph. In setting out the context of this chapter, the writer emphasizes the violence done to Joseph. He "was taken down" to Egypt. The Ishmaelites "brought him down there" (39:1). The same Hebrew verb, translated as "taken down" and "brought down," is repeated using an aspect that emphasizes being acted upon. The third verb in the sentence, *bought*, ("bought him from the Ishmaelites") reinforces that Joseph was a mere commodity in Egypt (v. 1).

There is a conflict between the details given in chapter 37 and those in this chapter. Verse 37:25 states that the brothers, once they had thrown Joseph in the waterless pit, "saw a caravan of Ishmaelites coming from Gilead." Judah proposes selling Joseph to the Ishmaelites (v. 27). However, it is Midianite traders who happen to pass by and take three actions: draw Joseph up, lift him from the pit, and sell him to the Ishmaelites (v. 28). The chapter concludes: "Meanwhile the Midianites had sold him [Joseph] in Egypt to Potiphar, one of Pharaoh's officials, the captain of the guard (v. 36).

It is apparent that the Midianites and Ishmaelites are two separate groups since the Midianites sell Joseph to the Ishmaelites. The final verse of chapter 37, however, clearly indicates that it is the Midianities who sell Joseph to Potiphar in Egypt. This detail is in conflict with the evidence presented in verse one of chapter 39. There, it is clearly the Ishmaelites who bring Joseph down to Egypt and sell him to Potiphar (39:1). Who sold Joseph, the Ishmalites or the Midianities?

This conflict is great fodder for a critic. Such conflict in detail is attacked as an example of the unreliability of the evidence presented. From the attack, the critic argues that all the testimony is suspect, since one is not sure of the accuracy of any given statement.

The writer is well aware of this line of attack. The writer, however, knows that a conflict in the evidence is always possible as it is presented. Humans do not tell the same story in the same way. Two people will tell different stories about the same observable events, and the same person may tell the same basic narrative in two different ways. An experienced investigator knows that when a story is told repeatedly in perfect detail or when two stories match in every detail, it is a sure indication that the truth is not being told. This story is full of conflicts in evidence. The issue for the reader is whether the conflict is relevant or not?

In this case, the important point for the narrative is that Joseph, against his will, is taken by force to Egypt and there sold as a slave. The name or race of the sellers is a detail of interest but not relevant to the narrative going forward. In such a carefully constructed story, this conflict points up the writer's full understanding of how people in their ordinary lives tell stories. He knows that humans never give perfect evidence and therefore, leaves the evidence as it is delivered. The writer has not scrubbed the evidence. The conflict left in place, however, does little to challenge the overall integrity of the narrative.

The reader is given three pieces of information about Potiphar. He is: a) an officer of Pharaoh, b) the captain of the guard, and c) an Egyptian. The first two pieces of information have already been given in Genesis 37:36. It is important that Potiphar is Egyptian because the reference raises the question of race. Potiphar is a native in Egypt, but Joseph is not. Race will be a consideration in this chapter and will play a role in the story of Jacob's family.

In 39:2 a new character is introduced: the Lord. As the story of Jacob's family starts out in Genesis 37, there is no mention of God. His name is not invoked, he does not appear, and he does not speak. The Lord does cause the death of Judah's two oldest sons, Er and Onan (38:7, 10), but Judah never understands this fact, and the Lord is otherwise absent from Tamar's story. The reader may surmise that Tamar has acted consistently with the Lord's will since she is blessed with twin sons. The reader may further suspect that the Lord sent the two dreams to Joseph but that is not made evident. In 39:2, the writer explicitly places the Lord directly into Joseph's life.

The text says, "The Lord was with Joseph" (39:2). The sense of this statement turns on the meaning of the Hebrew preposition translated as "with." The literal meaning suggests that the Lord is present with Joseph; the Lord has accompanied Joseph as he has been violently thrust into Egypt. Joseph is not alone in facing the ordeal of slavery.

The remaining part of verse 2 states that Joseph "became a successful man." The verb used for "successful" (*tsalach*) has the sense of "one who prospers" (*tsalach*). The verb is repeated in verse 3 and the explanation is given: "the Lord caused all that he did to prosper in his hands" (v. 3). The Lord has not only accompanied Joseph to Egypt but he is Joseph's ally. The Lord is "with" Joseph in the sense of actively promoting the well-being of Joseph, causing him to prosper. The Lord's presence is more than mere companionship but has real benefits in Joseph's life. Joseph "became a successful man; . . . . . the Lord caused all that he did to prosper," . . . "the Lord blessed the Egyptian's house for Joseph's sake" (vv. 2–5). All three of these boons come about because of the Lord.

The extent of the Lord's blessing is captured in the word *all*. In three verses, 39:3–6, the Hebrew text repeats the word "all" five times. The Lord intends Joseph to prosper without limitation. The Lord's blessing is abundant.

This success is recognized by Potiphar. "His master saw that the Lord was with him [Joseph]" (v. 3). Joseph is no longer a mere slave but has become the overseer of all Potiphar's property. The Lord's blessing is large, extending to his master's "house and field" (v. 5). All that Joseph does and everything he touches prospers.

Nothing is outside Joseph's control except "the food [Potiphar] ate" (v. 6). This qualification reasserts the issue of race. Later in the story the reader learns that it is an abomination for Egyptians to eat with others who are not Egyptian (43:32). Joseph's ability to make Potiphar prosperous is respected by the Egyptian. Potiphar, relying on Joseph's proven track record of success, trusts Joseph to be the manager of all Potiphar owns (v. 5). But Joseph remains a foreigner, a person apart from the Egyptians. Joseph is a slave. The prosperity flows to Potiphar. For the Egyptian, Joseph is merely the conduit.

No explanation is given for why the Lord is with Joseph. There is no suggestion that Joseph has done anything to merit this blessing. As with Jacob's favor, again Joseph is a beneficiary of an unearned blessing. Joseph does not even call on the Lord in prayer. For the first sixty-seven verses of the story there has been no indication that any members of Jacob's family are aware of the Lord's presence in their lives. Yet it is clear from the text that the

Lord has chosen to be with Joseph. It is the Lord who acts, the Lord who blesses.

The context for this passage has been set. Joseph is the successful overseer in the house of Potiphar, an Egyptian official. Not only is Joseph successful but he is also good looking (v. 6) The repetition of the Hebrew term for "beautiful" ("handsome and good-looking") adds distinct emphasis; Joseph is beautiful in form and beautiful in appearance. Joseph's success is manifested not only in his business dealings but also in his person. This is a beauty over which Joseph has no control. It is another aspect of the unearned blessing.

> Genesis 39:7–10
>
> [7]And after a time his master's wife cast her eyes on Joseph and said, 'Lie with me.' [8]But he refused and said to his master's wife, 'Look, with me here, my master has no concern about anything in the house, and he has put everything that he has in my hand. [9]He is not greater in this house than I am, nor has he kept back anything from me except yourself, because you are his wife. How then could I do this great wickedness, and sin against God?' [10]And although she spoke to Joseph day after day, he would not consent to lie beside her or to be with her.

Joseph's situation becomes fraught with danger when Potiphar's wife "casts her eye on Joseph" (v. 7). His beauty has been noticed. Potiphar's wife, like Judah seeing the assumed prostitute at Enaim, suffers from the same sexual desire. She orders Joseph, 'Lie with me' (v. 7). Joseph's problems arise from the reaction of others to him. Joseph's brothers misperceived him as a threat; Potiphar's wife misperceives Joseph as her personal property, a boy toy.

Joseph, unlike his brother Judah, does not suffer from overwhelming desires; an admirable quality in a handsome young man with whom the Lord is present. Joseph refuses the order of Potiphar's wife (v. 8) and then proceeds to explain his reasoning to the woman. This reasoning is an exposition on fiduciary law.

A fiduciary is one who holds and controls the property of another, for the benefit of the owner. The fiduciary does not own the property but has a duty of loyalty to the owner. The property should be managed for benefit of the owner, and not for the benefit of the fiduciary. This is a business relationship that involves trust. The word *fiduciary* comes from the Latin verb "to have confidence or trust."

The breach of a fiduciary duty is a variation on the analysis of a tort. In a fiduciary relationship, the breach occurs when the fiduciary acts for the benefit of himself or someone else. This is a breach of the duty of loyalty owed to the owner. The benefit, which should flow to the owner, after the breach, flows to another. This diversion of benefits is the damage caused by the breach of the duty of loyalty. The four elements of a tort exist in a breach of fiduciary duty—duty, breach, causation, and damages. The primary distinction between a fiduciary breach and an ordinary tort is the relationship of trust. The owner of a property trusts the fiduciary, and this trust must be known to the fiduciary for the relationship to exist.

In Joseph's case, Potiphar has entrusted "everything that he has" into Joseph's hand (v. 8). The Hebrew text repeats the term "all," meaning everything, recalling the earlier explanation of the extent of Joseph's control. But Joseph's control is for the benefit of Potiphar, the owner. Joseph is the fiduciary, trusted by Potiphar, to act for Potiphar's benefit. There are limits to Joseph's control. Joseph does not control Potiphar's wife (v. 9).

Potiphar's wife has proposed Joseph breach his fiduciary duty. She wants Joseph to act for her benefit rather than the benefit of Potiphar. The proposed breach is a form of theft. If Joseph were to be intimate with Potiphar's wife, he would take for his own benefit what belongs solely to Potiphar, Potiphar's consortium rights with his wife. Joseph refuses to obey the order.

This situation presents a sophisticated legal problem. Joseph is a slave. It is the very nature of slavery that the slave has no control over his person or the product of his labor. The slave's duty is to obey. Potiphar's wife demands obedience to her order. All of Egyptian society runs on the principle that slaves must obey their masters and mistresses.

To resolve the conflict, Joseph invokes a higher authority. He stands by his duty as a fiduciary and declares the wife's order, a "great wickedness." The outcome in this conflict between the two owners turns on Joseph's decision. "How then could I do this great wickedness?" (v. 9). And the second part in Hebrew reads: and [I] sin against God? Joseph is the decision-maker. He is no longer the seventeen-year-old carried against his will where he does not wish to go. Joseph, to some degree, has become his own man; he actively makes decisions concerning what he will or will not do. He chooses to be loyal to his master and also loyal to God. Joseph equates his duty of loyalty to his master Potiphar with his duty of loyalty to God. There is no suggestion that the two duties are in conflict.

Potiphar's wife has no interest in the nuances of fiduciary law. She continues to inveigle Joseph to lie with her (v. 9). Joseph remains firm in his refusal (v. 10). The Hebrew states he did not hear her, meaning he did not listen or obey. Unlike the wrongdoing in the earlier two chapters where there was a clear breach of duty, here there is a proposed breach of duty. In spite of Joseph's virtuous response, the immediate outcome is the same for Joseph.

> Genesis 39:11–12
>
> [11]One day, however, when he went into the house to do
> his work, and while no one else was in the house, [12]she
> caught hold of his garment, saying, 'Lie with me!' But he
> left his garment in her hand, and fled and ran outside.

When obedience is not forthcoming, Potiphar's wife pursues a course of self-help. She misperceives that Joseph is her property, and his duty is to obey his mistress. She acts to seduce him and thus compel his compliance.

She waits until she is alone with Joseph in the house. Being alone assures that there will be no witnesses to the seduction. It also offers Joseph the opportunity to hide his actions if he were to obey his mistress's order. Like Tamar, Potiphar's wife is a crafty strategist in carrying out her plan of self-help. The writer makes clear that Joseph is present in the house "to do his work" (v. 11).

He is not lurking in the loggia hoping that Potiphar's wife repeats her order.

But repeat the order she does. Potiphar's wife catches hold of Joseph's clothes and commands: 'Lie with me!' (v. 12). Joseph does three things: he abandons his clothes in his mistress's hand, he flees, and he goes out onto the street. Once again, others have rendered Joseph naked.

The last two verbs, to flee and to go out, make up a verbal coordination in Hebrew. The first verb acts as an adverb and the second verb shows the action; Joseph went out in a fleeing manner. This reading makes clear that Joseph immediately went out onto the street. He did not linger to analyze further the nuances of a fiduciary's duty of loyalty.

> Genesis 39:13-23
>
> [13]When she saw that he had left his garment in her hand
> and had fled outside, [14]she called out to the members of
> her household and said to them, 'See, my husband has
> brought among us a Hebrew to insult us! He came in to
> me to lie with me, and I cried out with a loud voice; [15]and
> when he heard me raise my voice and cry out, he left his
> garment beside me, and fled outside.' [16]Then she kept his
> garment by her until his master came home, [17]and she
> told him the same story, saying, 'The Hebrew servant,
> whom you have brought among us, came in to me to in-
> sult me; [18]but as soon as I raised my voice and cried out,
> he left his garment beside me, and fled outside.'
>
> 19 When his master heard the words that his wife
> spoke to him, saying, 'This is the way your servant
> treated me', he became enraged. [20]And Joseph's master
> took him and put him into the prison, the place where
> the king's prisoners were confined; he remained there
> in prison. [21]But the Lord was with Joseph and showed
> him steadfast love; he gave him favour in the sight of the
> chief jailer. [22]The chief jailer committed to Joseph's care
> all the prisoners who were in the prison, and whatever
> was done there, he was the one who did it. [23]The chief
> jailer paid no heed to anything that was in Joseph's care,

> because the Lord was with him; and whatever he did, the Lord made it prosper.

There are three consequences to Potiphar's wife's botched attempt at self-help. This section of the story repeats an interesting Hebrew grammatical structure; the Hebrew preposition *kaf* is used with the infinitive construct. The preposition indicates the precise time of the action, usually translated by "as soon as." In verse 13, the Hebrew reads: "when [as soon as] she [Potiphar's wife] saw that he [Joseph] left his clothes . . .". The writer has sped up the tempo of the narrative. There is a rush forward; action is taken immediately. Potiphar's wife encourages a rush to judgment. There is no attempt to stop and consider Joseph's side of the story.

First, Potiphar's wife realizes that her attempt at self-help has failed. Like Joseph's brothers at Dothan, she immediately begins to set out a narrative that will draw suspicion away from her. She calls out to the members of her household and tells them half-truths. These men are not witnesses, but Potiphar's wife hopes to shape their understanding so that they will support her side of the story (v. 14).

She starts by drawing attention to Joseph's race. He is a Hebrew. He is a foreigner, not like the other members of the household. Joseph has been brought among us . . . to insult us! (v. 14). The insult is probably the foreigner's refusal to respect the laws and customs of the host country. Foreigners are criminals. The Hebrew verb *tsachaq* means to laugh, translated by the idea to insult or mock. But it is also a word play on the name, Isaac, which means to laugh. The pun refers to Jacob's father.

After the race baiting, Potiphar's wife describes the alleged sexual assault. 'He came in to me [in order] to lie with me' which prompted her virtuous response: 'I cried out with a loud voice' (v. 14). The preposition *kaf* is again employed with the infinitive construct of the verb "to hear," to show that Joseph fled *as soon as* he realized Potiphar's wife was defending her virtue.

Finally, she presents her servants with physical evidence that corroborates her story. Joseph left behind his garment (v. 16). Like Joseph's brothers presenting Joseph's bloody coat to Jacob, Joseph's garment is used as physical evidence that is intended to mislead. She does not give an explanation for the clothes. The abandoned clothes suggest that Joseph may have disrobed as he initiated his assault. The rush to judgment does not allow consideration that Joseph was stripped of his clothing.

Potiphar's wife understands the importance of the physical evidence. There are no witnesses to corroborate her story but the physical evidence can be construed as support for her version of events. She keeps the clothing at hand until she can present it to her husband (v. 16).

When Potiphar comes home, his wife repeats almost the same story to her husband. First, she raises the issue of race. She does not name Joseph but refers to him as 'the Hebrew servant,' though the better term would be *slave*. She again blames Potiphar for having introduced the Hebrew into the household (v. 17).

An ambiguity arises in the Hebrew text. The text is translated he 'came in to me to insult me' (v. 17). The ambiguity is in the phrase "came in to me," and specifically the preposition *into*. These same words were used in chapter 38 to describe sexual intercourse. Onan is ordered to "go in to" Tamar (38:8). Judah negotiates to "come in to" Tamar (38:16). Is Potiphar's wife suggesting Joseph merely entered her presence, or that Joseph raped her? Both readings appear justified by the Hebrew text. Potiphar's wife intends her husband to draw the latter conclusion. The text reinforces this reading by concluding that Joseph's actions were 'to insult me' (v. 17), making the attack personal not directed at the Egyptian household.

The half-truths are repeated a second time; she immediately screams, he flees, clothes are abandoned (v. 18). There is no formal presentation of Joseph's clothing as evidence of the assault, but the reader knows Potiphar's wife has kept the clothes beside her (v. 16). One assumes Potiphar saw the clothes beside his wife as she told her tale and drew the conclusion she wanted from the evidence. She is a very effective advocate for her position.

Potiphar reacts immediately. The Hebrew reads: "When [As soon as] he heard" (v. 19). Potiphar rushes to judgment, which is to the great benefit of his wife. He condemns Joseph based on his wife's words. Joseph is put in prison (v. 20); he is naked in another pit (37:23–24). He has again been unjustly condemned.

The chapter concludes repeating many of the phrases from the beginning verses of the chapter. Joseph found favor in the eyes of Potiphar (39:4); Joseph found favor in the eyes of the chief jailer (v. 21). Potiphar gave into Joseph's hand all that he had (v. 5); the chief jailer gave into Joseph's hand all the prisoners and all that was done there (v. 22). Potiphar left all he had in Joseph's hands and "had no concerns for anything" (v. 6); "The chief jailer paid no heed to anything that was in Joseph's care" [literally, in his hands] (v. 23). Potiphar saw "that the Lord caused all that he [Joseph] did to prosper" (v. 3); the chief jailer concluded "whatever he [Joseph] did, the Lord caused it to prosper" (v. 23). The repetition neatly summarizes the situation at the end of this section of the story and ties the story together with the events described in the first verses of the chapter.

The writer tells the reader in verse two: The Lord was with Joseph. In verse 21, the writer states the Lord was with Joseph and then adds the further explanation "and [the Lord] showed him steadfast love." The Hebrew word *hesed* is here translated "steadfast love." The Hebrew word is used to describe one of the attributes of the Lord. (see Ps. 145:8–9) Holladay proposes the word *hesed* references loyalty, duties that arise in relationships; the obligation to the community.[10] Paired with the earlier discussion of the phrase "the Lord was with Joseph," the Lord has chosen to be in a relationship with Joseph and is undertaking to act for the benefit of Joseph. The Lord is causing Joseph's work to prosper. This is the loyalty the Lord extends to Joseph.

In the first three chapters of the story, the writer has set out three wrongs, or breaches of a recognized duty. It is now clear that each of these breaches is a breach of trust, a breach of fiduciary duty. First, Joseph trusts that his brothers will not harm him, but

10. William Lee Holladay and Ludwig Koehler, *A Concise Hebrew and Aramaic Lexicon of the Old Testament, based upon the lexical work of Ludwig Koehler and Walter Baumgartner* (Leiden, the Netherlands: E.J. Brill), #2710.

his brothers breach their duty of loyalty to him and do not act to protect his safety. Tamar trusts that Judah will provide her with a child, but Judah breaches his duty of loyalty to Tamar by sending her back to her father's house. Potiphar's wife aggressively urges Joseph to breach his duty of loyalty to his master. The breaches all concern human relationships, the duty one person owes to another or to his family. These wrongs are not breaches of humanity's duty to God. Except for Joseph's one reference in his discussion of fiduciary duty, the writer does not address the issue of sin, offense against God. The story of Jacob's family addresses human wrongdoing.

The world described in the story is not at peace. Literally, the fabric that holds society together, those myriads duties and benefits which we experience in a group and are woven together to provide social cohesion, is torn by these breaches, just as Tamar's flesh was torn by the birth of Perez. Trust is the element that allows humans to live together and advance. If family members, such as Joseph and Tamar, are unable to rely of the loyalty of their families, the world dissolves into chaos.

These breaches are known well at law. These wrongdoings are what Oliver Wendell Holmes, Jr. referred to when he spoke about experience being the life of the law. The law is very apt at recognizing wrongdoing and presenting an acceptable solution to the urge for vengeance that arises when the wrong is committed.

These breaches are examples of what Marilynne Robinson describes as humanity's "overwhelming bias toward error."[11] Humankind frequently and repeatedly makes mistakes; we get it wrong, we screw up. With the detailed description of the three breaches, the writer of the story of Jacob's family clearly establishes that humanity does not respect the duty of loyalty. Trust is breached, making it impossible for humanity to advance their true interests. The question then arises: Can these breaches be corrected?

The common law, as described by Holmes, seeks to answer that question. How does humankind redirect the urge for

11. Marilynne Robinson, *The Giveness of Things: Essays* (New York: Farrar, Straus and Giroux, 2015), 227.

vengeance? The first three chapters explore self-help as an option. In each chapter, there is a misperception of the truth. The self-help act is based on the misperception. The brothers see Joseph as a threat. They act on their misperception and lead the family into a pit of grieving. Judah misperceives the cause of his first two sons' deaths and acts to isolate Tamar. Potiphar's wife misperceives Joseph's duties as a slave and acts to impose her will. Humanity's bias to error includes errors in judgment.

Only Tamar, the outsider, understands the truth of her situation. She acts to correct the wrong done to her. Her restoration suggests a possible solution to the wrongs committed. One could simply restore the parties to their positions before the wrong was committed. But Tamar's case, and the experience of the common law, shows the severe limitations of this remedy.

With Joseph naked in a pit in chapter 37 and then naked and imprisoned in chapter 39, the writer suggests no remedy to the breaches that have caused Joseph damage. Wrong appears to prevail in Joseph's life. The issue raised by the first three chapters is what will allow humanity to go forward when it is so prone to wrong doing? If there is any hope for a better future, at this point in the story, it lies with the Lord who in chapter 39 is an acknowledged presence for the first time in Joseph's life. From this point forward, the writer sets out what it means for the Lord to be with Joseph and the rest of Jacob's family.

Three Restorations

Chapter 4

Joseph Elevated

Introduction

IN THE FIRST THREE chapters, when describing a breach of duty, the writer sets out the observable facts, the empirical evidence. The reader knows early in the story what actually happened. It is easy for the reader to see the truth of the matter when various actors try to obfuscate their intentions. For example, the reader knows that Joseph was not killed but that his brothers stood by while he was sold into slavery. The reader is also told the reason for the breach; the brothers were jealous. Except for the story of Judah and Tamar, the reader, however, is not shown a remedy for the breach, which is the fourth element in the modern tort action.

In this section, the writer addresses the issue of remedies. How can the family of Jacob go forward after they have breached their duty to a family member? In a larger context, how can humanity go forward when it has such a strong bias to error? As Holmes would have it, this is the basic question addressed by judges throughout the ages: What is the appropriate remedy so that the breach caused to the social fabric can be mended? Holmes uses an example from the book of Exodus (see Exod. 21:28)[12]

The better example for our purposes comes later in the same passage.

12. Holmes, *The Common Law*, 7.

> If someone's ox hurts the ox of another, so that it dies, then they shall sell the live ox and divide the price of it; and the dead animal they shall also divide. But if it was known that the ox was accustomed to gore in the past, and its owner has not restrained it, the owner shall restore ox for ox, but keep the dead animal (Exod. 21:35–36).

This passage nicely reflects the modern understanding of a tort. The owner with prior knowledge of goring has a duty to restrain his ox. If he breaches that duty causing damage to his neighbor's ox, then the owner of the vicious beast is liable for money damages to the injured party. The problem faced by the community is: a man's ox has been gored to death by his neighbor's ox which has a known history of goring. Moses sets out a remedy. The injured party gets a new ox of equal value to the one killed. The injured party is restored to his position prior to the breach. Moses presents a commonsense solution to an inevitable problem faced by his people. The remedy is an alternative to the very human desire for vengeance, in this case killing the offending ox, which can easily slide into the complete shattering of the social fabric. The remedy given by Moses is not an extended discussion of the sanctity of property rights. The remedy proposed is easily understood; it is workable in the parties' daily lives. For Holmes, it is of paramount importance that society has a shared sense that the given remedy heals the breach in an acceptable manner.[13]

Like Holmes' common law judge, the writer of the story of Jacob's family describes a remedy for the breach caused by Joseph's brothers. The issue before the reader in this section of the story is: What will restore the family of Jacob? But in setting out a solution to this problem, the writer moves beyond Oliver Wendell Holmes' survey of legal history. He goes beyond human justice. One suspects the writer has a vast experience concerning the tortfeasor's[14] liability for a goring ox. The story of Cain and Abel presents a

13. Holmes, *The Common Law*, 1–2.

14 A wrongdoer; an individual who commits a wrongful act that injures another and for which the law pro-vides *a legal right to* seek relief; a defendant in a civil tort action.

precedent on how to address the issue of a vengeful brother (4:1–16). Or one could look to the reunion of Jacob and Esau at the ford of the Jabbok (33:1–17). The brothers were sufficiently reconciled that they came together for the burial of their father. (35:29) These are very practical solutions to the problem of jealous brothers. The story of Jacob's family presents a possible solution in the precedent of Judah and Tamar. Judah acts honorably in human terms when he acknowledges his wrongdoing and restores Tamar to a position in his household. But this solution is only partial. There is no full reconciliation between Judah and Tamar (38:26).

Our writer moves beyond these precedents. We know that the Lord is with Joseph. In his life as a slave for Potiphar and later for the Prison Warden, the Lord's presence accounts for Joseph's highly accomplished skill as an administrator. These are very recognizable, human skills that one can see every day. The wise person acknowledges that common sense is not so common. Joseph is blessed with a good skill set for success in the Egyptian empire, and the Egyptians are very ready to exploit that skill set for their benefit.

But in chapter 40, the Lord's presence accounts for more than Joseph's very sought-after skill set. The Lord gives Joseph an extraordinary skill, one that cannot be explained in human terms. The writer is moving beyond the mundane. The writer is leading the reader to understand what God wants for Jacob's family. The issue for the writer is not to find a workable solution for the brothers' breach, the law proposes possible remedies, but rather to understand what God wants for this family.

To address this issue, the writer begins a more complicated analysis. Previously he simply told what happened and presented tangible evidence to bolster an actor's characterization of the evidence. The timeline for events was compacted; the reader knew the significance of events without a meaningful amount of time passing. In this chapter, the long-term consequences of a breach are not quickly explained to the reader; the writer's timeline is expanded. The reader is told what happens. But the significance of these actions is revealed to the reader in events that take place over a period of years. This extenuated narrative, where the reader does not see immediate consequences, reflects the realities of daily life for the readers. Often the consequences of an act are not known for years to come. It is difficult to know the truth, or the true significance of an act, until subsequent events over the years establish the event's meaning. Thus, the courts hate to speculate on a future outcome but rather address a breach when it has occurred. The courts, like all human institutions, are in no position to predict the future in any reliable fashion.

The nature of the evidence presented also changes in this chapter. Previously, the writer set out empirical evidence, observable facts that were easily understood. In this chapter, the writer turns from observable events to the description of dreams. The dreams tell of symbolic acts that are interpreted to represent future events. But it is only after some time has passed and events unfold that the truth of the dream is established. The reader is not able to determine the immediate meaning of a dream, but must wait along with the actors to see what happens next.

The writer has not moved to a supernatural world, where the laws of nature are upended. Everyone has dreams. It is a common experience, easily observed. It is the meaning of dreams that is not clear; the meaning is open to interpretation. The writer will provide an explanation of the dream's significance, but the fulfillment of the dream will occur in the natural world for all to see. There are no supernatural events in the story of Jacob's family except Jacob's vision in Genesis 32:22–32.[15] For example, the sun does not stop in the sky nor does an angel speak directly to Joseph or his brothers. The writer presents the reader with a clear understanding of the significance of an event through the dream interpretation, but the event foretold is ordinary. Everyone observes the same events unfold, proving the explanation to be correct, but the reader also understands the significance of the events.

In chapter 40, the writer begins to answer the question raised at Dothan, ". . .we shall see what becomes of his [Joseph's] dreams"

15. Jacob's "experience" of seeing angels ascending and descending a ladder to heaven come in a dream at the place he calls Bethel (Gen. 28:10–19).

(37:21). Joseph's dreams were described in chapter 37 without much explanation. In the following two chapters, 38 and 39, dreams were not present. In chapters 40 and 41, the writer returns to the theme of dreams and explains their power. These chapters are a subtle discussion of the nature of power. Understanding where true power lies, the writer can then explore a remedy to Joseph's situation.

Two Jailhouse Dreams

> Genesis 40:1–4
>
> Some time after this, the cupbearer of the king of Egypt and his baker offended their lord the king of Egypt. [2]Pharaoh was angry with his two officers, the chief cupbearer and the chief baker, [3]and he put them in custody in the house of the captain of the guard, in the prison where Joseph was confined. [4]The captain of the guard charged Joseph with them, and he waited on them; and they continued for some time in custody.

The context for this chapter's problem is given in the first verses. Joseph remains in prison (40:1–4). In verse 15 The NRSV refers to Joseph as being in a "dungeon." The Hebrew word used for *dungeon* is the same word translated as *pit*. It is the word used to describe Joseph's location at Dothan. At the beginning of chapter 40, Joseph's situation has not improved.

With Joseph are two officials from Pharaoh's court, the chief cupbearer and the chief baker. In verses 2–4 the word *chief* is used four times; a hierarchy is being established—chief cupbearer, chief baker, chief jailer, and Joseph, the Hebrew slave who is tasked with serving the two Egyptian officials (v. 4).

At the top of the power pyramid is Pharaoh, the greatest chief in the then known universe. His power is absolute. His officials have offended him (v. 1), he is angry with the two officials (v. 2), and as a consequence, he put them in custody in the prison where Joseph was confined (v. 3).

No reason is given for Pharaoh's anger. As a despot, no reason can be required of him. Perhaps it was merely Pharaoh's whim that the two officials be jailed. All three inmates, cupbearer, baker, and Joseph, may be suffering from an injustice. The writer makes no appeal to fairness or equity in this situation; he simply presents the men's condition. The reader, however, is sure that Joseph is not guilty of a crime. Joseph gives a resume of his situation in verse 15: 'I was stolen out of the land of the Hebrews; and here also I have done nothing that they should have put me into the dungeon [pit].'

> Genesis 40:5–18
>
> [5]One night they both dreamed—the cupbearer and
> the baker of the king of Egypt, who were confined in
> the prison—each his own dream, and each dream with
> its own meaning. [6]When Joseph came to them in the
> morning, he saw that they were troubled. [7]So he asked
> Pharaoh's officers, who were with him in custody in his
> master's house, 'Why are your faces downcast today?'
> [8]They said to him, 'We have had dreams, and there is no
> one to interpret them.' And Joseph said to them, 'Do not
> interpretations belong to God? Please tell them to me.'
>
> [9] So the chief cupbearer told his dream to Joseph,
> and said to him, 'In my dream there was a vine before
> me, [10]and on the vine there were three branches. As soon
> as it budded, its blossoms came out and the clusters rip-
> ened into grapes. [11]Pharaoh's cup was in my hand; and
> I took the grapes and pressed them into Pharaoh's cup,
> and placed the cup in Pharaoh's hand.' [12]Then Joseph said
> to him, 'This is its interpretation: the three branches are
> three days; [13]within three days Pharaoh will lift up your
> head and restore you to your office; and you shall place
> Pharaoh's cup in his hand, just as you used to do when
> you were his cupbearer. [14]But remember me when it is
> well with you; please do me the kindness to make men-
> tion of me to Pharaoh, and so get me out of this place.
> [15]For in fact I was stolen out of the land of the Hebrews;
> and here also I have done nothing that they should have
> put me into the dungeon.'

> 16 When the chief baker saw that the interpretation
> was favourable, he said to Joseph, 'I also had a dream:
> there were three cake baskets on my head, 17 and in the
> uppermost basket there were all sorts of baked food for
> Pharaoh, but the birds were eating it out of the basket on
> my head.' 18 And Joseph answered, 'This is its interpreta-
> tion: the three baskets are three days; 19 within three days
> Pharaoh will lift up your head—from you!—and hang
> you on a pole; and the birds will eat the flesh from you.'

The chapter's central problem arises when both officials have separate dreams that they do not understand (vv. 5–6). Joseph, as a good slave, observes their troubled faces and seeks to address the problem (vv. 6–7) The men explain they have dreamt but, 'there is no one to interpret them [their dreams]' (v. 8).

Joseph then addresses the problem with a rhetorical question, 'Do not interpretations belong to God?' (v. 8). Joseph raises the issue of where true power lies. It lies with God who alone knows the meaning of dreams. The impact of this power will be revealed in the lives of the three inmates.

Joseph further says to the officials, 'Please tell them [the dreams] to me' (v. 8). Joseph is in a new role. He has become the spokesperson for God. It is clear from the text that the power to understand the dreams lies with God. But Joseph is the one who expresses God's purposes to the Egyptians. It is not transparent how Joseph receives this understanding. Joseph does not have a vision nor does he receive a commission as did the later prophets (see, for example, Isaiah 6; Jer. 1:4–10). The modern reader at this point may consider Joseph a jailhouse lawyer, someone not licensed to practice law but based on his experience in the legal system, one who offers free advice to fellow prisoners. The value of the advice is yet to be determined.

Each dream is built around the number three. That number is repeated eight times in verses 10–20. This reinforces the structure of the entire story of Jacob's family.

The chief cupbearer tells his dream first. Joseph gives an interpretation: 'within three days Pharaoh will lift up your head and restore you to your office' (v. 13). The verb *lift* is used to indicate an elevation, a returning of honors.

Joseph's interpretation suggests that a dream is an indicator of what will come to pass. In the future, in three days precisely, the chief cupbearer will be restored. This foretelling is remarkable in its clarity and in its detail. Joseph is not telling of some vague future event that will occur at some unspecified future time, and therefore subject to various interpretations. Joseph is very specific. The reader will easily determine if the interpretation is true.

The ability to tell the future is an extraordinary skill. No human knows precisely what will happen tomorrow. Thus, there is no one to interpret the dreams of the Egyptian officials. The chances of correctly foretelling future events, no matter how vague, are extremely low. This is a high-risk situation for Joseph. If his interpretations do not come to pass his future will be in jeopardy.

To offer an interpretation testifies to Joseph's trust in the Lord. Joseph is sure that the Lord controls the future and has chosen Joseph to explain that future to his captors. The reader is not in a position to determine the truth of the dream when it is revealed. Future events will establish the validity of Joseph's interpretation. In three days, it will be evident whether this precise interpretation has become an observable reality.

Having addressed the chief cupbearer's problem, Joseph then pursues a course of self-help. He asks: 'please do me the kindness to make mention of me to Pharaoh, and so get me out of this place (v.14). The Hebrew word used here for kindness is *hesed*. This is the same word that described God's loyalty and steadfast love towards Joseph (39:21). Joseph is asking the chief cupbearer to show solidarity with a fellow prisoner who also suffers from a grave injustice. Joseph wants to be sprung from prison.

The chief baker, encouraged by Joseph's prognostication of the cupbearer's future, (v. 16), tells his dream. In the cupbearer's dream, there were three branches of grapes; compared to the three cake baskets on the baker's head. However, a bird eats the baked goods from the top basket (v. 17). Like a judge announcing a sentence in a criminal trial, Joseph declares, 'within three days

Pharaoh will lift up your head—from you!—and hang you on a pole; and the birds will eat the flesh from you' (v. 19). The verb *lift* in this case is used to show separation, not elevation. The word play works nicely in Hebrew and English.

> Genesis 40:20–23
>
> [20] On the third day, which was Pharaoh's birthday, he
> made a feast for all his servants, and lifted up the head
> of the chief cupbearer and the head of the chief baker
> among his servants. [21]He restored the chief cupbearer
> to his cupbearing, and he placed the cup in Pharaoh's
> hand; [22]but the chief baker he hanged, just as Joseph had
> interpreted to them. [23]Yet the chief cupbearer did not
> remember Joseph, but forgot him.

Three days after Joseph's interpretations, Pharaoh throws himself a birthday party and invites his court. Both the cupbearer and the baker are removed from prison. There are three consequences to Pharaoh's action. First, the cupbearer is restored (v. 21) to his position, but second, the baker is hanged (v. 22). No explanation is given for the two outcomes.

The third consequence concerns Joseph: "The chief cupbearer did not remember Joseph, but forgot him" (v. 23). The chief cupbearer fails to show solidarity with the Hebrew slave. Concerning the validity of Joseph's explanation, the writer concludes, events transpired "just as Joseph had interpreted to them" (v. 22).

A spirit of injustice hangs over the events of this chapter. No reason is given for Pharaoh's anger with his two officials. Joseph explains the two dreams, but he gives no rationale for the different consequences. The future of the two officials seems to be controlled by mere happenstance. The chief cupbearer reinforces the spirit of injustice by forgetting Joseph's kindness to him. For the moment, Joseph's extraordinary skill is of no use to the chief cupbearer.

Joseph's explanation of the dreams is proven to be valid by the events at Pharaoh's birthday party. Joseph is more than a jailhouse lawyer. While future events are controlled only by God, Joseph has the extraordinary power to explain through the interpretation of dreams what will happen before it occurs. The miracle is the ability accurately to foretell the future through the interpretation of dreams. When the future events occur, which are well within the bounds of empirical evidence, the reader is able to determine the remarkable accuracy of Joseph's skill. And at least one Egyptian (the cupbearer) is aware of what Joseph has done.

In the first three chapters, humanity suffered from repeated misperceptions; the actors do not understand the significance of the events that occur, draw the wrong conclusion, and then act on those bad judgments. Judah, for example, saw neither the truth of Tamar's situation during her marriages with his oldest sons, nor the person of Tamar sitting at the entrance to Enaim.

The events of chapter 40 establish that dreams are evidence of what God determines will occur. The revelation of God's intention removes one cause for humanity's profound propensity to get it wrong, to screw up. Hearing Joseph's interpretation, the reader has the means to understand what God will cause to happen. What God intends, as explained by Joseph, becomes the standard by which the reader judges what is true. This truth is firmly grounded in observable reality; it is not a vague, philosophical construct of what should be. Focusing on God's intentions, humanity avoids the pitfalls of misperceiving the significance of events.

This leads the reader back to Joseph's two dreams in chapter 37 at the very beginning of the story. Joseph has two dreams, one of the brothers' sheaves bowing down to Joseph's sheaf, and a second dream of the spangled heavens bowing down to Joseph. The events in chapter 40 confirm that dreams properly interpreted are a valid indication of future events, and the reader can look back and conclude that the Lord proposes a better outcome for Joseph than that of the chief baker. The Lord intends Joseph to reign over the family of Jacob. The family was right to be astonished at Joseph's audacity.

Joseph's audacity and extraordinary skill, however, have yet to be fully realized. At the end of chapter 40, that extraordinary power is ignored and Joseph remains in the pit.

A Double Dream

> Genesis 41:1–8
>
> After two whole years, Pharaoh dreamed that he was
> standing by the Nile, [2]and there came up out of the Nile
> seven sleek and fat cows, and they grazed in the reed
> grass. [3]Then seven other cows, ugly and thin, came up
> out of the Nile after them, and stood by the other cows
> on the bank of the Nile. [4]The ugly and thin cows ate up
> the seven sleek and fat cows. And Pharaoh awoke. [5]Then
> he fell asleep and dreamed a second time; seven ears of
> grain, plump and good, were growing on one stalk. [6]Then
> seven ears, thin and blighted by the east wind, sprouted
> after them. [7]The thin ears swallowed up the seven plump
> and full ears. Pharaoh awoke, and it was a dream. [8]In the
> morning his spirit was troubled; so he sent and called for
> all the magicians of Egypt and all its wise men. Pharaoh
> told them his dreams, but there was no one who could
> interpret them to Pharaoh.

As chapter 41 begins, Joseph is still in jail. His situation has not changed for two years (41:1). Pharaoh himself then has two dreams. Fortunately, the writer tells us later in the chapter that the two dreams are one and the same (v. 25). This clarifies the narrative structure around the number three. There are four dreams that Joseph is asked to explain—the chief cupbearer's, the chief baker's, and two dreamt by Pharaoh; but the last two describe one future event, making, in effect, three dreams. The writer remains on the well-hewn path by continuing to build his argument around the number three.

There is much repetition in this chapter. The dreams of Pharaoh are described by the writer, and then Pharaoh repeats almost the same descriptions to Joseph. The writer also explains the importance of this repetition. "The doubling of Pharaoh's dreams means that the thing is fixed by God and will shortly bring it about" (v. 32). The repetition in the story helps to fix important details in the listener's mind. The first 36 verses of chapter 41 with all its repetitions tell about one event. From the perspective of plot, this is the most important event in the entire story All the rest of the chapters (42–50) are a working out of the consequences of this event.

Pharaoh has a dream. The pattern established in chapter 40 is again followed in chapter 41: the dream is told; there is no one to interpret; Joseph is proposed as an interpreter; Joseph gives an explanation; Joseph proposes a plan of self-help. Chapter 41 adds two consequences to the pattern.

The writer starts by setting out the events in Pharaoh's first dream. There are seven sleek and fat cows grazing along the Nile (v. 2). Seven ugly and thin cows come out of the Nile and eat up the first group (vv. 3–4) In the second dream, there are seven plump and good ears of grain on one stalk (v. 5); then seven thin and blighted ears sprout and eat the former (vv. 6–7). The parallels in the two dreams are obvious: sleek and fat / plump and good; ugly and thin / thin and blighted; ate up / swallowed.

No one among all the magicians of Egypt can interpret these dreams for Pharaoh. (v. 8). This is understandable since no rational human would want to take the risk of precisely predicting future events; such power lies beyond the grasp of humanity. Failure in the interpretation would mean sharing the fate of the chief baker.

> Genesis 41:9–24
>
> 9 Then the chief cupbearer said to Pharaoh, 'I remember
> my faults today. 10 Once Pharaoh was angry with his
> servants, and put me and the chief baker in custody in
> the house of the captain of the guard. 11 We dreamed on
> the same night, he and I, each having a dream with its
> own meaning. 12 A young Hebrew was there with us, a
> servant of the captain of the guard. When we told him,
> he interpreted our dreams to us, giving an interpretation
> to each according to his dream. 13 As he interpreted to us,
> so it turned out; I was restored to my office, and the baker
> was hanged.'
>
> 14 Then Pharaoh sent for Joseph, and he was
> hurriedly brought out of the dungeon. When he had
> shaved himself and changed his clothes, he came in
> before Pharaoh. 15 And Pharaoh said to Joseph, 'I have

> had a dream, and there is no one who can interpret it. I have heard it said of you that when you hear a dream you can interpret it.' [16]Joseph answered Pharaoh, 'It is not I; God will give Pharaoh a favourable answer.' [17]Then Pharaoh said to Joseph, 'In my dream I was standing on the banks of the Nile; [18]and seven cows, fat and sleek, came up out of the Nile and fed in the reed grass. [19]Then seven other cows came up after them, poor, very ugly, and thin. Never had I seen such ugly ones in all the land of Egypt. [20]The thin and ugly cows ate up the first seven fat cows, [21]but when they had eaten them no one would have known that they had done so, for they were still as ugly as before. Then I awoke. [22]I fell asleep a second time and I saw in my dream seven ears of grain, full and good, growing on one stalk, [23]and seven ears, withered, thin, and blighted by the east wind, sprouting after them; [24]and the thin ears swallowed up the seven good ears. But when I told it to the magicians, there was no one who could explain it to me.'

It finally dawns on the chief cupbearer that he has already had the same experience of no one to explain his dream. The chief cupbearer repeats his experience to Pharaoh: We [cupbearer and baker] dreamed; there was a Hebrew slave; we told him the dreams; he interpreted; the dreams were proven true (vv. 11–13). 'As he interpreted to us, so it turned out' (v. 13). The chief cupbearer establishes the pattern for this section of the narrative: dream, confusion, Joseph explains, and events establish the truth of the explanation. The reader anticipates that each of these elements will be fulfilled.

Pharaoh sends for Joseph (v. 14). Joseph does three things: a) he shaves, b) he changes his clothes, and c) he goes into Pharaoh's presence. The three actions are an indication that things are looking up for Joseph. He is old enough to shave, as he is no longer a stripling but a full man, and he gets himself cleaned up. He is not stripped of his clothing, but of his own volition changes his clothes and is properly dressed. Joseph is being recognized as a person with some dignity. He enters Pharaoh's presence, a place of the highest prestige, and he is not brought in against his will. Joseph, finally, is out of the pit (v. 14).

Pharaoh tells Joseph that he has been summoned to explain Pharaoh's dreams. Joseph makes clear from the beginning that the power to interpret dreams lies with God. 'It is not I; God will give Pharaoh a favorable answer' (v. 16). True power lies with God, not with Pharaoh. Like a good counselor, Joseph is bending the narrative in his client's favor. He has yet to hear the dream, but he is already promising that Pharaoh will be pleased with his explanation. Advice is easier to accept and act on when it promises a benefit to the recipient.

Pharaoh tells Joseph his dream. Pharaoh's version, however, differs from what the writer has already set out. Witnesses seldom tell the same facts in exactly the same way. Pharaoh adds details when speaking to Joseph. The thin and ugly cows become in Pharaoh's telling "poor, very ugly and thin" (v. 19). He adds the adjective "poor" and then the further detail, "Never had I seen such ugly ones in all the land of Egypt" (v. 19). The action in the dream remains the same: the seven good cows are eaten, but Pharaoh adds the detail, ". . .no one would have known they [the thin and ugly cows] had done so, for they were still as ugly as before" (v. 21). The thin and blighted ears of grain become "withered, thin and blighted" (v. 23); Pharaoh adds another adjective, "withered." They swallow up the good ears. Pharaoh's elaborations emphasize the harshness of his dreams.

> Genesis 41:25–36
>
> 25 Then Joseph said to Pharaoh, 'Pharaoh's dreams are
> one and the same; God has revealed to Pharaoh what he
> is about to do. 26 The seven good cows are seven years, and
> the seven good ears are seven years; the dreams are one.
> 27 The seven lean and ugly cows that came up after them
> are seven years, as are the seven empty ears blighted by
> the east wind. They are seven years of famine. 28 It is as
> I told Pharaoh; God has shown to Pharaoh what he is
> about to do. 29 There will come seven years of great plenty
> throughout all the land of Egypt. 30 After them there will

> arise seven years of famine, and all the plenty will be for-
> gotten in the land of Egypt; the famine will consume the
> land. [31]The plenty will no longer be known in the land
> because of the famine that will follow, for it will be very
> grievous. [32]And the doubling of Pharaoh's dream means
> that the thing is fixed by God, and God will shortly bring
> it about. [33]Now therefore let Pharaoh select a man who
> is discerning and wise, and set him over the land of
> Egypt. [34]Let Pharaoh proceed to appoint overseers over
> the land, and take one-fifth of the produce of the land
> of Egypt during the seven plenteous years. [35]Let them
> gather all the food of these good years that are coming,
> and lay up grain under the authority of Pharaoh for food
> in the cities, and let them keep it. [36]That food shall be a
> reserve for the land against the seven years of famine that
> are to befall the land of Egypt, so that the land may not
> perish through the famine.'

Joseph explains the dreams to Pharaoh. They foretell a single event. Through his dreams, "God has shown to Pharaoh what he is about to do" (v. 28). The action lies with God. There will be seven years of abundant harvest followed by seven years of "very grievous" famine (v. 31).

Joseph then sets out a six-point strategic plan to address this crisis, "so that the land may not perish through the famine" (v. 36). He says that Pharaoh should:

1. Seek an able counselor (an attorney?);
2. Put him in charge of Egypt;
3. Appoint overseers, a tax bureaucracy;
4. Collect twenty percent of Egypt's annual food production during the good years;
5. Store the grain under Pharaoh's authority; and
6. Use the stored grain for food in the cities during the famine.

This six point plan is well beyond the normal self-help scenarios already seen in the story of Jacob's family. In this case, Joseph is proposing a plan that will carry out God's judgment as evidenced in Pharaoh's double dream. The reader knows what God intends to happen through the interpretation of the dream. Joseph proposes the means to make that intention a reality.

Three Actions by Pharaoh

Genesis 41:37–45

> [37] The proposal pleased Pharaoh and all his servants.
> [38]Pharaoh said to his servants, 'Can we find anyone else
> like this—one in whom is the spirit of God?' [39]So Pha-
> raoh said to Joseph, 'Since God has shown you all this,
> there is no one so discerning and wise as you. [40]You shall
> be over my house, and all my people shall order them-
> selves as you command; only with regard to the throne
> will I be greater than you.' [41]And Pharaoh said to Joseph,
> 'See, I have set you over all the land of Egypt.' [42]Removing
> his signet ring from his hand, Pharaoh put it on Joseph's
> hand; he arrayed him in garments of fine linen, and put
> a gold chain around his neck. [43]He had him ride in the
> chariot of his second-in-command; and they cried out
> in front of him, 'Bow the knee!' Thus he set him over all
> the land of Egypt. [44]Moreover, Pharaoh said to Joseph, 'I
> am Pharaoh, and without your consent no one shall lift
> up hand or foot in all the land of Egypt.' [45]Pharaoh gave
> Joseph the name Zaphenath-paneah; and he gave him
> Asenath daughter of Potiphera, priest of On, as his wife.
> Thus Joseph gained authority over the land of Egypt.

Pharaoh adopts Joseph's six-point plan and appoints him to carry it out. Pharaoh explains his decision saying, 'Since God has shown you all this, there is no one so discerning and wise as you' (v. 39). Joseph, straight out of prison, has only explained Pharaoh's dream. It will take at least eight years to prove that the interpretation is accurate. Pharaoh's confidence in Joseph seems more a whim than a well-reasoned decision. The fate of the chief baker should be kept in mind.

Pharaoh attributes Joseph's power to God, but there is no recognition by Pharaoh of God's sovereignty. Pharaoh is content to benefit from Joseph's relationship with God but fails to pay more than lip service to God's power over the future.

Pharaoh's trust in Joseph has echoes of both Potiphar's and the Prison Warden's trust in Joseph. Between verses 37 and 44 in chapter 41, the word *all* is used six times to explain Joseph's authority. This same language was used to describe Joseph's authority in chapter 39. Joseph has control over Pharaoh's house (41:40), just as he had authority over Potiphar's house (39:4), and just as he had complete authority over the entire prison (39:22). Joseph's authority over Egypt is summarized in verse 44. By Pharaoh's order no one shall lift hand or foot in all the land of Egypt without Joseph's consent. Though he has great power, ultimately the Egyptians will exploit Joseph's gifts for their own benefit.

There is, however, another element of trust in the story that falls outside the purview of the master's trust in the slave. Joseph has trusted in God. How Joseph learns of God's will is never explained. But when Joseph learns God's intentions, he tells others. Joseph has very real experience of the high-risk dangers of dream interpretation. If Joseph had been more mature he likely would not have told his dreams to his brothers. It was Joseph's naivete in telling his dreams that landed him in slavery.

Joseph now finds himself before the most powerful ruler in the world. If Joseph has misunderstood God's will or falters in the explanation, his fate is probably sealed like that of the chief baker. At some point in time while in Egypt, Joseph came to understand that his only hope was the Lord. Only God, through the gift of interpretation, provides the means for Joseph to escape from the pit. There is no rational explanation for Joseph's gift, except that it comes from the Lord. Joseph trusts the Lord and stakes his life on it.

Pharaoh's appointment goes far beyond Joseph's previous positions of trust. These verses emphasize great exuberance. Joseph is in control of "all the land of Egypt" (v. 41). This authority is shown in three gestures. Joseph is given the signet ring from Pharaoh's hand, some special clothes, and a gold chain to be worn around the neck (v. 42). The clothes remind the reader of the special robe

Jacob gave Joseph (37:3). All three items also recall Judah's pledged items to Tamar (38:18). The three items given by Pharaoh are tangible evidence of Joseph's authority. All the world knows that Pharaoh has chosen Joseph as his prime minister.

Joseph's authority is put in place by three orders from Pharaoh. Joseph will ride in the chariot behind Pharaoh, a place of highest honor. Second, Joseph's arrival will be announced by the order 'Bow the knee!' (v. 43), and Joseph will have complete authority over all activities in Egypt (v. 44).

Finally, Pharaoh gives Joseph back his life. Joseph is given a new name (v. 45) and thus becomes a recognized member of Egyptian society. He is given an Egyptian wife and she bears him sons (vv. 50–52). Joseph summarizes his situation by saying 'For God has made me fruitful . . .' (v. 52).

All of these good things come to Joseph because the Lord is with him. Joseph's extraordinary skill establishes that the Lord is truly with Joseph in a unique way. Joseph's previous success in Potiphar's house could be attributed to his natural gifts. There is nothing natural about the power to interpret dreams. That power only comes from God. Joseph's success can only be attributed to the Lord. It is clear that God controls events and has turned them to benefit Joseph. Pharaoh is merely an actor who, unknowingly, carries out God's will. True sovereignty lies with the Lord.

Three Actions by Joseph

Genesis 41:46–57

46 Joseph was thirty years old when he entered the service
of Pharaoh king of Egypt. And Joseph went out from the
presence of Pharaoh, and went through all the land of
Egypt. 47 During the seven plenteous years the earth pro-
duced abundantly. 48 He gathered up all the food of the
seven years when there was plenty in the land of Egypt,
and stored up food in the cities; he stored up in every city
the food from the fields around it. 49 So Joseph stored up

> grain in such abundance—like the sand of the sea—that
> he stopped measuring it; it was beyond measure.
> 50 Before the years of famine came, Joseph had two
> sons, whom Asenath daughter of Potiphera, priest of On,
> bore to him. 51 Joseph named the firstborn Manasseh,
> 'For', he said, 'God has made me forget all my hard-
> ship and all my father's house.' 52 The second he named
> Ephraim, 'For God has made me fruitful in the land of
> my misfortunes.'
> 53 The seven years of plenty that prevailed in the land
> of Egypt came to an end; 54 and the seven years of famine
> began to come, just as Joseph had said. There was fam-
> ine in every country, but throughout the land of Egypt
> there was bread. 55 When all the land of Egypt was fam-
> ished, the people cried to Pharaoh for bread. Pharaoh
> said to all the Egyptians, 'Go to Joseph; what he says to
> you, do.' 56 And since the famine had spread over all the
> land, Joseph opened all the storehouses, and sold to the
> Egyptians, for the famine was severe in the land of Egypt.
> 57 Moreover, all the world came to Joseph in Egypt to buy
> grain, because the famine became severe throughout the
> world.

Given a free hand, Joseph proceeds to implement his strategic plan in two phases. First, the harvest is abundant (v. 47). Joseph collects food and has it stored in the cities. (v. 48). It is a time of plenty, the earth produces abundantly, the harvest "was beyond measure" (v. 49).

This spirit of abundance comes to an abrupt halt after seven years with the arrival of famine in the land, "just as Joseph had said" (v. 54). This calls for Joseph to implement the second phase of his action plan, the people of Egypt are fed (v. 56). Joseph's interpretation of Pharaoh's double dream has been proven valid. The extent of the famine is overwhelming in its harshness. The word *all* is repeated eight times in the last three verses of the Hebrew text. Not only Egypt experiences a famine, but all the world experiences a food shortage (v. 57).

Joseph has acted based on his trust in the Lord. Joseph does not sit passively in Pharaoh's court telling anyone who will listen about his prognostications, awaiting the Lord to act. Just as Tamar acted to fulfill the Lord's intention for her life (chapter 38) Joseph goes out and prepares for the future. His trust leads to action. He uses his wonderful skill set as an administrator to prepare for the crisis he knows will come.

Joseph's two-phase plan works. The purpose of the plan is to preserve the land of Egypt, 'so that the land may not perish through famine' (41:36). When the Egyptians come to Pharaoh demanding food, he directs them to Joseph (v. 55). Joseph sells the Egyptians grain from the storehouses (v. 56). Moreover, foreigners from outside Egypt come to Joseph to buy grain (v. 57).

Joseph, is thirty years old (41:46) when he is elevated over Pharaoh's household; for the Egyptians his authority is practically an apotheosis. He is seventeen at the beginning of the story (37:2). Joseph was a slave for thirteen years. The text does not describe Joseph's suffering during this time. Perhaps those to whom the story was originally told had a clear idea of the fate of slaves, since it was an everyday situation. The psalmist describes Joseph's situation in this way:

> When he [the LORD] summoned famine
>   against the land,
> and broke every staff of bread,
> he had sent a man ahead of
>   them,
> Joseph, who was sold as a
>   slave.
> His feet were hurt with fetters,
> his neck was put in a collar of
>   iron;
> Until what he said came to
>   pass,
> The word of the LORD kept
>   testing him. (Ps 105:16–19)

Joseph must have been physically and mentally wounded by his slavery. He gives some indication of his suffering with the third action he takes in this chapter, the naming of his two sons. The eldest is named, Manasseh, 'For,' he said, 'God has made me forget all my hardship and all my father's house' (v. 51). By referencing the hardships and his father's house, Joseph has clearly not forgotten these things. The second son is named Ephraim, 'For God has made me fruitful in the land of my misfortunes' (v. 52). All the exuberance of his apotheosis has not removed the pain of his situation. He remembers his suffering. Joseph is not at peace in Egypt.

Chapters 40 and 41 begin to provide an answer to the question at Dothan, "we shall see what will become of his dreams" (37:20). They establish that dreams have the power to foretell future events. Those future events are controlled by God. The reader can now look back and realize that Joseph's two dreams, described in chapter 37, have begun to come true. Metaphorically with his appointment to control all of Egypt, the most powerful nation in the world, Joseph's sheaf has arisen and stood upright (see 37:7).

The problem of Joseph being in a pit has been resolved. Joseph is allowed to act on his volition. The injustice of Potiphar of putting Joseph in prison is simply not addressed. Pharaoh's wishes override Potiphar's misplaced anger.

Joseph's restoration, however, is not a return to the past. Joseph is not freed from slavery, he does not travel back to Hebron, and his return is not celebrated by his father Jacob with the fatted calf. Joseph is restored to something new. He is a person of power in Egypt. God's plan requires Joseph to move toward something new, not return to Jacob's household.

Joseph enjoys great material blessing because of the Lord's presence with him. But it would be wrong to see this as merely an example of the prosperity gospel. Joseph also suffers. Having the Lord present did not protect Joseph from injustice. The Lord did not free Joseph from slavery. The Lord's presence eventually rectified the injustice of Potiphar but it did not spare Joseph anguish. The Lord is steadfastly loyal, but that loyalty does not provide ever flowing blessing.

Joseph's life in Egypt as Pharaoh's prime minister is an incomplete restoration. The events at Dothan not only harmed Joseph, but they shattered the peace of Jacob's family. That peace has yet to be restored. Joseph's present plan calls for actions to save the land of Egypt during the famine. The following chapters address God's purposes during this crisis.

With the conclusion of chapter 41, there is a pause in the narrative action. There is a break in the story's timeline. With chapter 42, the scope of the action moves from Joseph to include Jacob's entire family, and the context moves from Joseph's presence in Egypt to Canaan, Joseph's homeland.

Chapter 5

The Brothers Restored

THE FOLLOWING VERSES PROVIDE a further answer to the question asked at Dothan: What will become of Joseph's dreams? The writer in this section follows the narrative pattern established in chapters 37, 38, and 39: a trip by Joseph's brothers leads to trouble, just as Joseph's trip to find his brothers had led to trouble for him. A second trip ends with a possible restoration, similar to Judah's trip to the sheep shearing. And finally there is an implacable injustice, as Joseph suffered with Potiphar.

The First Trip to Egypt

Genesis 42:1–14

When Jacob learned that there was grain in Egypt, he
said to his sons, 'Why do you keep looking at one another? 2I have heard', he said, 'that there is grain in Egypt;
go down and buy grain for us there, that we may live and
not die.' 3So ten of Joseph's brothers went down to buy
grain in Egypt. 4But Jacob did not send Joseph's brother
Benjamin with his brothers, for he feared that harm
might come to him. 5Thus the sons of Israel were among
the other people who came to buy grain, for the famine
had reached the land of Canaan.

> 6 Now Joseph was governor over the land; it was
> he who sold to all the people of the land. And Joseph's
> brothers came and bowed themselves before him with
> their faces to the ground. [7]When Joseph saw his brothers,
> he recognized them, but he treated them like strangers
> and spoke harshly to them. 'Where do you come from?'
> he said. They said, 'From the land of Canaan, to buy
> food.' [8]Although Joseph had recognized his brothers,
> they did not recognize him. [9]Joseph also remembered
> the dreams that he had dreamed about them. He said to
> them, 'You are spies; you have come to see the naked-
> ness of the land!' [10]They said to him, 'No, my lord; your
> servants have come to buy food. [11]We are all sons of one
> man; we are honest men; your servants have never been
> spies.' [12]But he said to them, 'No, you have come to see
> the nakedness of the land!' [13]They said, 'We, your ser-
> vants, are twelve brothers, the sons of a certain man in
> the land of Canaan; the youngest, however, is now with
> our father, and one is no more.'
>
> [14]But Joseph said to them, 'It is just as I have said to
> you; you are spies!'

The context for this chapter is revealed at the end of chapter 41: "The famine became severe throughout the world" (41:57). This famine extends as far as the family of Jacob in the land of Canaan. Jacob knows there is grain in Egypt and sends ten of his sons to Egypt in order to buy provisions (vv. 1–2). Jacob's purpose, 'that we may live and not die' (v. 2), is consistent with the goal of Joseph's strategic plan: 'so that the land may not perish through famine' (41:36).

In seeking provisions, however, Jacob has become wiser. Benjamin, the youngest and, like Joseph, a son born to Rachel (35:24), does not go down to Egypt with his ten brothers. The brothers have a history of losing Jacob's favorite child. Jacob "feared that harm might come to him [Benjamin]" (v. 4). The actors in the story are beginning to behave more astutely. They more accurately understand the situation in which they find themselves and take measures to protect their interests. And perhaps the reader may be relieved for the moment, knowing the same fate will not befall the youngest of Jacob's sons.

This first trip to Egypt echoes many of the events in chapter 37. At the beginning of the story, the same ten brothers go to Shechem and then to Dothan to find food for Jacob's flock. This time the brothers go to Egypt to find food for Jacob's family (v. 5).

In Egypt, as at Dothan, Joseph is present. The Hebrew verb for *recognized* is used three times in verses 7 and 8. Joseph recognizes the brothers, but they fail to recognize him. Just as earlier in the story the brothers misperceived Joseph as a threat to what they think is their entitlement, now they misperceive with whom they are dealing. Joseph does not correct the misperception. Like Tamar at the entrance to Enaim (39:14–15), Joseph's identity remains hidden.

Joseph speaks harshly to his brothers, treating them like strangers (v. 7). The stage is set for vengeance. Joseph has suffered for thirteen years because of these ten men and is now in a position to pay them back. All humanity, in every corner of this celestial ball, recognizes this urge for revenge. It is so fundamental that Justice Holmes sees it as the beginning of any analysis of liability, sanctions imposed by the law.[16] The reader anticipates that Joseph will apply the eye-for-an-eye principle later enunciated by Samson, "As they did to me, so I have done to them" (Judg. 15:11). The reader awaits a story of Joseph wreaking vengeance.

It will take some time before the writer completely resolves the reader's anticipation. Joseph's initial reaction to his brothers' presence is to remember his dreams (v. 9). This memory offers at least a hope that Joseph will not wreak total devastation on his brothers. He needs the brothers alive to fulfill the dreams, to bow down to him. Joseph showed in his first meeting with Pharaoh that he trusted God's revelation of the future as revealed in Pharaoh's dreams and Joseph acts on that trust. Now he must trust the dreams he had when he was seventeen years old. When the ten brothers bow themselves before him [Joseph] with their faces

16. Holmes, *The Common Law*, 2.

to the ground (v. 6), the dream of the sheaves is partially fulfilled, but with one brother missing, the complete fulfillment must wait.

Joseph takes three actions concerning his brothers. He starts by questioning them. For the first time in the story, someone challenges an assertion that has been made. In Chapter 37 Jacob does not question the origin or circumstances surrounding the presentation of Joseph's bloody robe. Jacob could have asked: How did the brothers find the robe? Where specifically was it found? Was there no other evidence of Joseph at the site? Jacob does not test the truth of the evidence provided by the brothers, but rather leaps to the conclusion that Joseph has been devoured by a wild animal (37:33). Later, Potiphar repeats the same error and does not challenge the evidence of Joseph's clothing that his wife propounds. Misleading evidence abounds in this story.

On their first trip to Egypt, Joseph challenges his brothers. It is only in challenging an assertion that the truth is revealed; details are elicited, facts not originally expressed are brought to light, and clarifications are established. In American law this questioning is called cross-examination. It is the opportunity for the accused to confront his accuser and to ask him questions. To be cross-examined is never a pleasant experience, but history shows it to be an effective vehicle to discover the truth.

Joseph's cross-examination has three stages. Joseph starts by asking about the brothers' native land. They are from Canaan and want to buy food (v. 7). Second, Joseph declares that the brothers are spies, "come to see the nakedness of the land!" (v. 9). As Joseph was naked and vulnerable in the pit at Dothan, so now he asserts that the brothers are trying to determine the vulnerability of Egypt when it is naked of crops. The brothers respond by asserting they are honest men, the sons of one father, in Egypt to buy food, and not spies (v. 11).

Joseph re-asserts that they are spies. This assertion elicits more details. The cross-examination is effective. The ten men before Joseph are twelve brothers in total, all the sons of one man in Canaan. One of the twelve has died and the youngest stayed at home (v. 13). Joseph ends the cross examination by concluding, "you are spies!" (v. 14).

> Genesis 42:15–25
>
> 15Here is how you shall be tested: as Pharaoh lives, you shall not leave this place unless your youngest brother comes here! 16Let one of you go and bring your brother, while the rest of you remain in prison, in order that your words may be tested, whether there is truth in you; or else, as Pharaoh lives, surely you are spies.' 17And he put them all together in prison for three days.
>
> 18 On the third day Joseph said to them, 'Do this and you will live, for I fear God: 19if you are honest men, let one of your brothers stay here where you are imprisoned. The rest of you shall go and carry grain for the famine of your households, 20and bring your youngest brother to me. Thus your words will be verified, and you shall not die.' And they agreed to do so. 21They said to one another, 'Alas, we are paying the penalty for what we did to our brother; we saw his anguish when he pleaded with us, but we would not listen. That is why this anguish has come upon us.' 22Then Reuben answered them, 'Did I not tell you not to wrong the boy? But you would not listen. So now there comes a reckoning for his blood.' 23They did not know that Joseph understood them, since he spoke with them through an interpreter. 24He turned away from them and wept; then he returned and spoke to them. And he picked out Simeon and had him bound before their eyes. 25Joseph then gave orders to fill their bags with grain, to return every man's money to his sack, and to give them provisions for their journey. This was done for them.

Joseph responds to his brothers' appearance before him by cross-examining them. His second action is to set his brothers a test. One brother will go back to Canaan to fetch the youngest brother, Benjamin, and bring him back to Egypt. The remaining nine brothers will be held hostage in Egypt (v. 15). The youngest brother's presence in Egypt will establish the truth of his siblings' testimony (v. 16). The test assumes the brothers have a bedrock commitment to protecting each other, that the brothers are loyal one to another and one brother will not leave the other brothers rotting in an Egyptian prison. These same men have previously violated this bedrock loyalty in the case of Joseph at Dothan. The reader may question whether the brothers will again cut their losses and abandon the hostages in Egypt.

Joseph carries out his test. The brothers are put in prison. Having traveled from their home in Canaan, the brothers, again, get into trouble.

On the third day, Joseph softens his judgment. One brother will be held hostage in Egypt, while the others will be allowed to travel to Canaan and then bring back the youngest (vv. 19–21). There is a blessing in Joseph's new decree. The brothers are allowed to "carry grain for the famine of your households" (v. 19). Jacob's family will survive. The return of Benjamin will confirm—literally "amen"—the brothers' testimony (v. 20). They must prove that their testimony is reliable. This testing is the goal behind the cross-examination; it verifies the truth.

The brothers misperceive the situation. They tell each other that their anguish results from their earlier bad treatment of Joseph (v. 21). They are telling themselves a tale of vengeance. The word *anguish* is repeated twice, once for Joseph's anguish when he was sold into slavery and the other time to describe the brothers' suffering in the Egyptian prison. The brothers are setting up a reciprocal relationship between what they did in the past and their present suffering. This is the basic concept behind society's understanding of justice, it is reciprocal or retributive. Justice requires that the guilty party receive a punishment that is appropriate, or fits, the nature of the crime.

Proving that even older brothers can be irritating to their younger siblings, Reuben points out that he had told his brothers at Dothan, before Joseph was sold, that this would happen (v. 22; compare to 37:21–22). He repeats the age-old complaint of the eldest, "But you would not listen" (v. 22). He recalls the prohibition on shedding blood (v. 22; compare to 37:22) further tightening the structural references between chapter 37 and chapter 42. Rueben also affirms the reciprocal nature of the brothers' perspective. Rueben believes there will be a reckoning for Joseph's poor treatment at the hands of the brothers (v. 22). The brothers have admitted they had a duty to protect Joseph and that they breached that duty (v. 21). Tort law, and the brothers' reasoning, demand that the brothers assume liability for their action and that punishment be meted out or damages be paid.

Joseph further softens the severity of the situation by turning aside and weeping. (v. 24). Joseph's weeping is a theme in the last half of this story. There is no weeping by Joseph during his thirteen years as a slave; that freedom comes only with his elevation into Pharaoh's household. Different situations cause Joseph to weep. In this case, he weeps out of empathy with the fear displayed by his brothers. His feelings, however, do not stop him from executing his plan. Simeon is selected as the hostage, and bound before his brothers' eyes (v. 24b). Joseph was lost at Dothan and now Simeon is held hostage in Egypt.

After cross-examining his brothers and taking one as hostage, Joseph's third action is to order his brothers' bags to be filled with grain and "to return every man's money to his sack and to give them provisions for their journey" (v. 25). The harsh treatment of the brothers is again tempered by Joseph's outpouring of grain. There is a famine in all the world, yet Joseph not only gives food for the households back in Canaan, but also food for the journey. And it is all free! The native Egyptians were not treated so well. Joseph sold Pharaoh's grain to Pharaoh's own people, the ones who raised the grain and paid the tax (41:56).

> Genesis 42:26–38
>
> 26 They loaded their donkeys with their grain, and
> departed. 27 When one of them opened his sack to give his
> donkey fodder at the lodging-place, he saw his money at
> the top of the sack. 28 He said to his brothers, 'My money
> has been put back; here it is in my sack!' At this they lost
> heart and turned trembling to one another, saying, 'What
> is this that God has done to us?'

> 29 When they came to their father Jacob in the land
> of Canaan, they told him all that had happened to them,
> saying, 30 ‘The man, the lord of the land, spoke harshly
> to us, and charged us with spying on the land. 31 But we
> said to him, “We are honest men, we are not spies. 32 We
> are twelve brothers, sons of our father; one is no more,
> and the youngest is now with our father in the land of
> Canaan.” 33 Then the man, the lord of the land, said to us,
> “By this I shall know that you are honest men: leave one
> of your brothers with me, take grain for the famine of
> your households, and go your way. 34 Bring your youngest
> brother to me, and I shall know that you are not spies but
> honest men. Then I will release your brother to you, and
> you may trade in the land.” ’
>
> 35 As they were emptying their sacks, there in each
> one’s sack was his bag of money. When they and their
> father saw their bundles of money, they were dismayed.
> 36 And their father Jacob said to them, ‘I am the one
> you have bereaved of children: Joseph is no more, and
> Simeon is no more, and now you would take Benjamin.
> All this has happened to me!’ 37 Then Reuben said to his
> father, ‘You may kill my two sons if I do not bring him
> back to you. Put him in my hands, and I will bring him
> back to you.’ 38 But he said, ‘My son shall not go down
> with you, for his brother is dead, and he alone is left. If
> harm should come to him on the journey that you are to
> make, you would bring down my grey hairs with sorrow
> to Sheol.’

There are three consequences to the brothers’ encounter with Joseph. First, one of them discovers his money at the top of the grain sack when they stop for the night. All ten react with dismay and “turned trembling to one another” (v. 28). In their fear they ask, ‘What is this that God has done to us?’ (v. 28b). Their question is not as simple as it appears in English. The Hebrew grammar reflects an enclitic use of the demonstrative, *this*. It is the way Hebrew language curses. One could politely render the idea by “what the devil has God done to us?” The seventeen-year-old Holden Caulfield would use more profane language.

The brothers misperceive the situation. In their minds, the brothers anticipate a reckoning for their great wrong against Joseph. They are afraid because they know that they merit punishment. The law should impose damages for their tort. They attribute this retributive justice to God. In this paradigm, which is the model for daily life in any society, they will get what they deserve.

The facts of the situation do not bear out this conclusion. The brothers have received an extraordinary gift—free food during a famine. No word of condemnation has been uttered. Joseph has set his brothers a test. The brothers wrongly anticipate the outcome. The brothers believe they can foresee what will happen. For them, it will not be good. The reader, however, through the events in Joseph's life, knows that the future belongs to the Lord alone.

The second consequence to meeting Joseph is the report the brothers must bring back to Jacob. In Chapter 37 the brothers did not give any specifics about their time away from home, but merely presented a bloody robe (37:32). Here they must repeat the details of their encounter with the "lord of the land" (v. 30). It is a very honest report, accurately setting out what was said, except that they add the promise that they will be allowed to trade in Egypt (v. 34). There was no discussion of trade in their encounter with Joseph. All witnesses edit their testimony. The challenge of cross examination is to nail down the specifics. The brothers, however, are getting better at accurately presenting the facts of their situation.

The third consequence is that Jacob and his sons discover that all the money has been returned (v. 35). They react with dismay as they did at the lodging-place (v. 35). Jacob believes that he is the nucleus of the situation. 'All this has happened to me!' (v. 36). Jacob also misconstrues the situation; he anticipates disaster in spite of the fact that the family has received great blessing in the food and money.

Reuben's efforts to console his father prove ineffective. Jacob will not allow Reuben to take Benjamin back to Egypt in order to free Simeon (v. 38). Reuben, who was ineffective at rescuing Joseph at Dothan (37:29–30), drew the wrong conclusion about a reckoning in Egypt (42:22) and will not be allowed to rescue

Simeon from Egypt (v. 38). Reuben, the eldest, is clearly not the right candidate to lead Jacob's family into the future.

Chapter 37 ends with Jacob foreseeing his descent to Sheol (37:35). Chapter 42 also ends with Jacob foreseeing the possibility that his grey hair will go down to Sheol with sorrow (v. 38). There is fear and trembling throughout Jacob's family in Canaan. Certainly, there is no peace and the family's well-being continues to be threatened by the famine.

The Second Trip

Genesis 43:1–14

Now the famine was severe in the land. [2]And when they
had eaten up the grain that they had brought from Egypt,
their father said to them, 'Go again, buy us a little more
food.' [3]But Judah said to him, 'The man solemnly warned
us, saying, "You shall not see my face unless your brother
is with you." [4]If you will send our brother with us, we
will go down and buy you food; [5]but if you will not send
him, we will not go down, for the man said to us, "You
shall not see my face, unless your brother is with you."
' [6]Israel said, 'Why did you treat me so badly as to tell
the man that you had another brother?' [7]They replied,
'The man questioned us carefully about ourselves and
our kindred, saying, "Is your father still alive? Have
you another brother?" What we told him was in answer
to these questions. Could we in any way know that he
would say, "Bring your brother down"?' [8]Then Judah said
to his father Israel, 'Send the boy with me, and let us be
on our way, so that we may live and not die—you and we
and also our little ones. [9]I myself will be surety for him;
you can hold me accountable for him. If I do not bring
him back to you and set him before you, then let me bear
the blame for ever. [10]If we had not delayed, we would now
have returned twice.'

11 Then their father Israel said to them, 'If it must
be so, then do this: take some of the choice fruits of the
land in your bags, and carry them down as a present to

> the man—a little balm and a little honey, gum, resin, pistachio nuts, and almonds. [12]Take double the money with you. Carry back with you the money that was returned in the top of your sacks; perhaps it was an oversight. [13]Take your brother also, and be on your way again to the man; [14]may God Almighty grant you mercy before the man, so that he may send back your other brother and Benjamin. As for me, if I am bereaved of my children, I am bereaved.'

As foretold in Pharaoh's dream, the famine is very severe and Jacob's family eventually runs out of food (vv. 1–2). Jacob has three responses to the crisis. First, he orders his sons back to Egypt (v. 2). Judah comes forward as the leader of the brothers. Judah refuses his father's order unless Benjamin travels with the older men. Judah twice repeats Joseph's threat, 'You shall not see my face unless your brother is with you.' (vv. 3 and 5). The repetition emphasizes the spirit of menace that hangs over the family. The brothers understand they have no power over the lord of the land.

Jacob in his second response does not concede control of the situation to Judah. Jacob has no interest in bowing before one of his son's dictates, 'If we had not delayed, we would now have returned twice' (v. 10). Jacob (Israel) blames his sons for the threat to Benjamin (v. 6). Judah defends his actions by explaining how the situation transpired. 'The man questioned us carefully' (v. 7). This is the essence of cross examination, to ask questions carefully. The use of the adverb *carefully* suggests Joseph was not merely carrying on a conversation but was seeking information from the brothers. The astute observer follows the sequence of the questions asked. An attorney calls this following the line of questioning. In following the line of questioning, the reader begins to see the direction in which the questions are moving and thus reveals the questioner's true subject of inquiry. In Egypt, Joseph asked "about ourselves and our kindred" (v. 7). The real interest of the man in Egypt is the family of Jacob, not a commercial transaction to buy grain.

Judah offers himself as surety for Benjamin's safe return (v. 9). Judah clearly understands his obligation. 'If I do not bring him back to you and set him before you, then let me bear the blame for ever' (v. 9). Judah is placing his future within the confines of tort law. The Hebrew word used for *surety* is the same word Judah used for a *pledge* when negotiating with Tamar (38:18). Judah is again in the middle of a commercial transaction. In Chapter 38 he negotiates for the prostitute's services. In Chapter 43, he prepares to negotiate for more food from Joseph and the safe passage of Benjamin.

Jacob's third response is to set out the structure of the commercial transaction that will acquire more food in Egypt. He is very experienced with commercial transactions. Jacob went toe to toe and bested his uncle Laban in Genesis 29 and 30, as each tried to out manoeuver the other in various commercial transactions. Jacob also knows the value of gifts. He sent extravagant gifts to Esau from Mahanaim (Gen. 32:13-15) in order to win his estranged brother's favor.

Jacob has a three-point action plan to win over the lord of the land. He prepares gifts, "choice fruits of the land" (v. 11) for this stranger. The list of gifts recalls the items carried by the Ishmaelite traders (see Gen. 37:25). In addition to the gifts, Jacob directs his sons to take double the money, thus paying for the first shipment and having funds for a second shipment. Third, he allows Benjamin to accompany his brothers (v. 13).

Genesis 43:15–25

[15]So the men took the present, and they took double the
money with them, as well as Benjamin. Then they went
on their way down to Egypt, and stood before Joseph.

[16] When Joseph saw Benjamin with them, he said to
the steward of his house, 'Bring the men into the house,
and slaughter an animal and make ready, for the men are
to dine with me at noon.' [17]The man did as Joseph said,
and brought the men to Joseph's house. [18]Now the men
were afraid because they were brought to Joseph's house,
and they said, 'It is because of the money, replaced in
our sacks the first time, that we have been brought in, so
that he may have an opportunity to fall upon us, to make
slaves of us and take our donkeys.' [19]So they went up to

> the steward of Joseph's house and spoke with him at the
> entrance to the house. [20]They said, 'Oh, my lord, we came
> down the first time to buy food; [21]and when we came to
> the lodging-place we opened our sacks, and there was
> each one's money in the top of his sack, our money in
> full weight. So we have brought it back with us. [22]More-
> over, we have brought down with us additional money
> to buy food. We do not know who put our money in our
> sacks.' [23]He replied, 'Rest assured, do not be afraid; your
> God and the God of your father must have put treasure
> in your sacks for you; I received your money.' Then he
> brought Simeon out to them. [24]When the steward had
> brought the men into Joseph's house, and given them
> water, and they had washed their feet, and when he had
> given their donkeys fodder, [25]they made the present
> ready for Joseph's coming at noon, for they had heard
> that they would dine there.

The brothers return to Joseph with the three items—gifts, money, and Benjamin. This is their second trip to Egypt. Joseph gives three orders in response to his brothers' return. The men are to be taken to Joseph's house, a meal is to be prepared, and the men are to dine with Joseph at noon (v. 16). These commands are all blessings.

The brothers react with fear (v. 18) They again misperceive the situation. The brothers reason, 'It is because of the money, replaced in our sacks the first time, that we have been brought in' (v. 18). They think they are being isolated in order to harm them because of the money that was returned (v. 18). The brothers continue to believe the lord of the land is interested in a commercial transaction. They fail to understand that their fate will be decided under a different rubric. The brothers' fear is based on three conjectures about their isolated presence in Joseph's house: the Egyptians will overpower them, make them slaves, and take their donkeys (v. 18) This is exactly what happened to Joseph when his disloyal family abandoned him at Dothan.

Misperceiving both the nature of their present situation and its cause, the brothers seek to suborn Joseph's steward. They set out a six-point explanation of why they are being falsely judged, which also serves to remind the listener of the important plot points in the brothers' situation. Their first trip was to buy food, but they discovered the returned money after they left and they have returned with this money. Furthermore, they have come back with additional money to buy more food; the return of the first money was an unforeseen mishap. They are explaining the outline of a commercial transaction whose purpose is to buy grain.

Joseph's steward has a three-point reply to this misunderstanding: be not afraid; your God has provided; the payment was received (v. 23). Remarkably, the Egyptian steward brings a word of peace and witnesses to the providence of God. The outsider steward sees the truth of the matter. The steward's loyalty is to Joseph and his duty is to carry out Joseph's orders. He will not get involved in further helping the ten brothers. He does, however, bring out the captive Simeon (v. 23). The brothers are reunited with the hostage. Now, eleven brothers wait for Joseph.

The steward then acts to implement Joseph's original order. He brings the men into Joseph's house, provides water for them to wash, and gives fodder for their donkeys (v. 24). Everything is taken care of, the hostage is free, and the brothers are met with kindness; even the well-being of the pack animals is addressed. The brothers have every reason to rejoice.

The brothers then turn their attention to the pending commercial transaction. They prepare the gift for Joseph. Just as Judah sought to buy Tamar's favor at the entrance to Enaim in chapter 38, so the brothers in chapter 43 seek to carry out Jacob's strategy for a successful commercial transaction by winning Joseph's favor with their gift (v. 25).

Genesis 43:26–34

> [26] When Joseph came home, they brought him the present that they had carried into the house, and bowed to the ground before him. 27He inquired about their welfare, and said, 'Is your father well, the old man of whom you spoke? Is he still alive?' 28They said, 'Your servant our father is well; he is still alive.' And they bowed their heads and did obeisance. 29Then he looked up and saw

> his brother Benjamin, his mother's son, and said, 'Is
> this your youngest brother, of whom you spoke to me?
> God be gracious to you, my son!' 30With that, Joseph
> hurried out, because he was overcome with affection
> for his brother, and he was about to weep. So he went
> into a private room and wept there. 31Then he washed
> his face and came out; and controlling himself he said,
> 'Serve the meal.' 32They served him by himself, and
> them by themselves, and the Egyptians who ate with him
> by themselves, because the Egyptians could not eat with
> the Hebrews, for that is an abomination to the Egyptians.
> 33When they were seated before him, the firstborn ac-
> cording to his birthright and the youngest according to
> his youth, the men looked at one another in amazement.
> 34Portions were taken to them from Joseph's table, but
> Benjamin's portion was five times as much as any of
> theirs. So they drank and were merry with him.

Joseph comes home, the brothers present their gift "and bow to the ground before him" (v. 27). The pronoun *they* refers to the eleven brothers, the *him* is Joseph. The dream of the sheaves, set out in chapter 37:7 has been fulfilled. The brothers are bowing to Joseph who has clear dominion over them. The Lord set out his intentions in the dream in Canaan and those intentions have been fulfilled in Egypt.

Is this not enough? In chapters 40 and 41 the dreams of the cupbearer, baker, and Pharaoh were explained and in the allotted time, events proved the explanation to be true. There was no partial fulfillment of the Egyptian dreams. "As he interpreted to us, so it turned out" (41:13). The fulfillment of Joseph's dreams will not be this simple.

Joseph responds to the brothers' presence with three questions. First, he asks about their welfare, about his father's welfare (v. 27) and finally asks, 'Is this your younger brother, of whom you spoke to me?' (v. 28). Joseph's questions guide the reader to the real issue, the welfare of Jacob's family. Joseph is not interested in a commercial transaction.

Before an answer to the last question is given, Joseph hurries out of his brothers' presence and goes into a private room to weep (v. 30). The writer explains that he is "overcome with affection for his brother, [Benjamin]" (v. 30). Joseph then reverses himself, as Tamar did when she resumed her position as a widow. He washes his face, returns to his brothers, and controls himself (v.31).

Then Joseph orders the meal served. There are three separate locations for the food service. Joseph sits by himself, showing his position of authority. The brothers sit opposite him at their own table. Protocol is respected. The eldest, Rueben, is given the place of honor; Benjamin, the youth, receives the last seat (v. 33). There is a third group in the room—the Egyptians who have been invited. The Egyptians eat at their own table, "because the Egyptians could not eat with the Hebrews, for it was an abomination to the Egyptians" (v. 32). The arrangement reminds the reader that the Hebrews are in a foreign land. Life is very good for Joseph but he is not a fully accepted member of Egyptian society.

The meal suggests reconciliation. All the sons of Jacob are together sharing a meal. Under the law of reciprocal justice, this reconciliation is the best outcome one could reasonably anticipate. There was misunderstanding and anguish in the past, but the meal suggests a way forward. In chapter 38, Tamar was restored to Judah's house. In Chapter 43 the sons of Jacob appear, in human terms, to be reconciled. The brothers start out their visit to Joseph's house being afraid (v. 18). The chapter concludes with the brothers' amazement (v. 33). They anticipated anguish but instead received a banquet. The past appears to be left behind.

Moreover, the brothers appear to have matured in their thinking. They are seated according to rank; oldest to youngest. But it is the youngest who receives the most honor. Benjamin's portion is five times greater than any of his brothers (v. 34). In chapter 37 such preferential treatment would have been cause for hatred and jealousy among the brothers. At the banquet, no one questions Benjamin's special status, rather, "they drank and were merry with him" (v. 34). All that is lacking is the conclusion: they lived happily ever after.

The Third Trip

Genesis 44:1–5

Then he commanded the steward of his house, 'Fill the
men's sacks with food, as much as they can carry, and put
each man's money in the top of his sack. [2]Put my cup, the
silver cup, in the top of the sack of the youngest, with his
money for the grain.' And he did as Joseph told him. [3]As
soon as the morning was light, the men were sent away
with their donkeys. [4]When they had gone only a short
distance from the city, Joseph said to his steward, 'Go,
follow after the men; and when you overtake them, say
to them, "Why have you returned evil for good? Why
have you stolen my silver cup? [5]Is it not from this that
my lord drinks? Does he not indeed use it for divination?
You have done wrong in doing this." '

The happy ending of chapter 43 is short-lived. The writer understands the realities of daily life that happy endings can be fleeting. Morning arrives after the banquet, and it bodes ill for the brothers. The events of the first trip to Egypt recounted in chapter 42 were foreshadowed by the events in chapter 37, ending with Jacob in Sheol. The confrontation between Judah and Tamar in chapter 38 ending with Tamar's partial restoration is a harbinger of events during the second trip to Egypt concluding with the banquet at Joseph's house. The brothers, after the banquet, soon leave Joseph and begin their journey home. The trip is cut short in chapter 44. They make a third trip to Joseph. Chapter 39, with its theme of implacable injustice, foreshadows the brothers' third trip to Joseph.

As Potiphar's wife plotted to trap Joseph, so Joseph plots to entrap his brothers. The trap alleges a theft. Potiphar's wife wants Joseph to steal her husband's consortium rights. In this passage, Joseph fraudulently suggests the theft of his silver cup. He gives his steward three orders that will lay the trap. 'Fill the men's sacks with food, as much as they can carry' (v. 1). This is an extravagant gift during a famine. Second, return each man's money (v. 1). This is the double portion that the brothers brought at their father's insistence, another extravagance. Third, place the silver cup in Benjamin's sack (v. 2).

The brothers leave Joseph by dawn's early light. After a brief time, Joseph orders his steward to go in hot pursuit of them. Joseph gives the steward three questions to pose to his brothers: Why did you return evil for good? Why did you steal the silver cup? Is this not Joseph's cup from which he drinks and divines? (vv. 4–5). The questions go from a general observation to the specifics of the case.

The question, why did you return evil for good, is an overarching theme throughout the book of Genesis. It starts with Adam and Eve in the Garden and goes forward from there. The good is the garden where God places humanity, but Adam and Eve do not stay there. They fail to respect God's goodness but chose to do what they perceive to be in their interest. The question of returning evil for good reflects Marilynne Robinson's observation that humanity has an overwhelming propensity to get it wrong, to make the wrong choice, to misperceive the situation.[17]

The first three chapters of the story of Jacob's family give no clear answer to the question of what will be the consequences for those who return evil for good. The beginning of the story describes wrongdoing, how humanity misperceives the true significance of a situation. So far in the story, the writer has not addressed what will be the reckoning for this wrongdoing.

Having asked his questions, the steward is instructed to conclude, "You have done wrong in doing this" (v. 5). The entrapment is based on a retributive view of justice. If you do wrong, then you should be punished. Joseph is entrapping the brothers with their own concept. Since coming to Egypt the brothers believe their troubles are caused by their past wrongs (42:21). With the entrapment, even false charges of wrong lead to punishment. The entire world has turned against the brothers. There is no succor in truth or justice for the eleven men. The brothers have fallen into

17. Marilynne Robinson, *The Givenness of Things* (New York: Farrar, Straus and Giroux, 2015), 227.

the same situation as Joseph, who was ensnared by the lies of Potiphar's wife, in chapter 39.

> Genesis 44:6–13
>
> [6] When he overtook them, he repeated these words to them. [7]They said to him, 'Why does my lord speak such words as these? Far be it from your servants that they should do such a thing! [8]Look, the money that we found at the top of our sacks, we brought back to you from the land of Canaan; why then would we steal silver or gold from your lord's house? [9]Should it be found with any one of your servants, let him die; moreover, the rest of us will become my lord's slaves.' [10]He said, 'Even so; in accordance with your words, let it be: he with whom it is found shall become my slave, but the rest of you shall go free.' [11]Then each one quickly lowered his sack to the ground, and each opened his sack. [12]He searched, beginning with the eldest and ending with the youngest; and the cup was found in Benjamin's sack. [13]At this they tore their clothes. Then each one loaded his donkey, and they returned to the city.

The steward carries out his mission and overtakes the brothers on their journey back to Canaan (v. 6). The writer does not repeat Joseph's three questions. The questions are not important. The writer wants the reader to focus on the reaction of the brothers.

The outcome for the brothers is organized around three oaths or exclamations. Unlike Joseph in chapter 39, the brothers are allowed to make a defense. When confronted by the steward's accusations, the brothers respond with wonder, 'Far be it from your servants that they should do such a thing!' (v. 7). Other translations use the phrase "God forbid." The brothers mount a very good defense. They have already proven they are honest. They returned the first payment. There is no reason for them to turn dishonest in Joseph's house (v. 8). This defense works nicely in a commercial transaction. They then double down on their oath. If the accusation is proved true, let the thief die and the remaining ten become slaves (v. 9) This is the first oath.

The steward replies with his own oath, the second in the passage (v. 10). The steward answers that only the thief will be punished, and the rest can go on their way. It is a core tenet in the retributive justice system that only the guilty party merits an appropriate punishment. An innocent party may not be tainted with another's guilt. The brothers lower their sacks, open them, and the steward begins searching, starting with the oldest and proceeding in order (v. 11). The planted evidence is found in Benjamin's sack (v. 12).

The brothers show great solidarity with Benjamin. All the brothers return to Joseph (v. 13). Under the steward's oath, only the thief was to be apprehended. The older men could have gone on their way. But the brothers remain loyal to Benjamin and by implication to their father, Jacob, who is waiting anxiously in Canaan. Perhaps they fear the Egyptian's wrath less than they fear having to tell their father that Benjamin is now lost to him.

> Genesis 44:14–17
>
> [14] Judah and his brothers came to Joseph's house while
> he was still there; and they fell to the ground before him.
> [15]Joseph said to them, 'What deed is this that you have
> done? Do you not know that one such as I can practise
> divination?' [16]And Judah said, 'What can we say to my
> lord? What can we speak? How can we clear ourselves?
> God has found out the guilt of your servants; here we are
> then, my lord's slaves, both we and also the one in whose
> possession the cup has been found.' [17]But he said, 'Far be
> it from me that I should do so! Only the one in whose
> possession the cup was found shall be my slave; but as for
> you, go up in peace to your father.'

The brothers enter Joseph's presence for a third time. Joseph repeats the false accusation: what have you done? (v. 15). Judah no longer has a defense. The brothers are in the same position as Joseph in chapter 39 before the prison warden. The injustice is implacable. Judah responds to Joseph's accusation with three questions. These same questions may have been in Joseph's mind when Potiphar threw him in prison. What can we say? What words could we use?

How can we clear ourselves? (v. 16). The injustice is overwhelming. The brothers are crushed. They declare themselves to be Joseph's slaves (v. 16). They have become like Joseph in Potiphar's house, a slave. The brothers throw themselves on the mercy of the court.

Joseph ends the brothers' defense with the third oath. 'Far be it from me that I should do so!' The oath echoes the one made by the brothers when confronted by Joseph's steward; they were inordinately sure of their innocence. Joseph declares that only the thief will be detained. The others may return to their father (v. 17).

Genesis 44:18–34

> [18] Then Judah stepped up to him and said, 'O my lord,
> let your servant please speak a word in my lord's ears,
> and do not be angry with your servant; for you are like
> Pharaoh himself. [19]My lord asked his servants, saying,
> "Have you a father or a brother?" [20]And we said to my
> lord, "We have a father, an old man, and a young brother,
> the child of his old age. His brother is dead; he alone is
> left of his mother's children, and his father loves him."
> [21]Then you said to your servants, "Bring him down to
> me, so that I may set my eyes on him." [22]We said to my
> lord, "The boy cannot leave his father, for if he should
> leave his father, his father would die." [23]Then you said
> to your servants, "Unless your youngest brother comes
> down with you, you shall see my face no more." [24]When
> we went back to your servant my father we told him the
> words of my lord. [25]And when our father said, "Go again,
> buy us a little food", [26]we said, "We cannot go down. Only
> if our youngest brother goes with us, will we go down; for
> we cannot see the man's face unless our youngest brother
> is with us." [27]Then your servant my father said to us, "You
> know that my wife bore me two sons; [28]one left me, and I
> said, Surely he has been torn to pieces; and I have never
> seen him since. [29]If you take this one also from me, and
> harm comes to him, you will bring down my grey hairs
> in sorrow to Sheol." [30]Now therefore, when I come to
> your servant my father and the boy is not with us, then,
> as his life is bound up in the boy's life, [31]when he sees
> that the boy is not with us, he will die; and your servants

> will bring down the grey hairs of your servant our father with sorrow to Sheol. [32]For your servant became surety for the boy to my father, saying, "If I do not bring him back to you, then I will bear the blame in the sight of my father all my life." [33]Now therefore, please let your servant remain as a slave to my lord in place of the boy; and let the boy go back with his brothers. [34]For how can I go back to my father if the boy is not with me? I fear to see the suffering that would come upon my father.'

Judah then steps forward for a side-bar discussion with Joseph: 'let your servant please speak a word in my lord's ear' (v. 18). A side-bar discussion occurs during a jury trial when an attorney asks the judge to approach the bench so that the attorney may give the judge information outside the hearing of the jury. Judah wishes to speak to Joseph outside the hearing of the Egyptians and his brothers. It is his hope to reason quietly with Joseph and to avoid Joseph posturing to show his power before the others.

In his side-bar discussion, Judah seeks to reframe the issue. So far, the brothers have acted on the assumption that Joseph is concerned with a commercial transaction. The brothers believe the lord of the land wants to receive what he is owed in money and to recover his stolen cup. Judah's initial defense was based on the brothers' rigorous respect for the obligations of the commercial transaction. Finally, Judah begins to address the issue that is of utmost interest to Joseph; the status of Jacob's family. The astute reader has understood this concern because of the direction taken in Joseph's questions. The emphasis in Judah's side-bar is on the relationships within Jacob's family. Judah is beginning to understand the real issue.

Judah starts with the information elicited in the brothers' first encounter with Joseph (see 42:7–13) At home are their father, an old man and their youngest brother. The youngest's full brother is dead and consequently the father dearly loves the youngest (v. 20). Judah repeats Joseph's order from the first encounter; 'Bring him [the youngest] down to me' (v. 21). The brothers answer that sending the boy would kill the father. This warning is an addition to the story in chapter 42 but emphasizes the importance of family relationships. In Judah's narrative, it does not dissuade Joseph and he renews his demand (v. 22).

Judah continues his narrative. Time passes and the food runs out (see 43:1–10). This time Jacob issues the order to buy more food (v. 25). The brothers bring up the necessity of Benjamin accompanying them and repeat Joseph's threat (v. 26). Jacob reviews his predicament; he has two favored sons but only one is left. The loss of the youngest son would be an insurmountable sorrow to Jacob (v. 29).

After this review, Judah states two conclusions, indicated by the phrase, "Now therefore". These are the same words an attorney uses at the end of his written argument, what follows is the summary of Judah's argument. Judah has set out the facts in his review. He then, as a good advocate, sets out his prayer, stating exactly how he wants the lord of the land to rule. Perhaps the judge's mind has wandered or he has become lost in the details of the argument. The advocate, at the end of his presentation, summarizes indicated by the words "now therefore," telling the judge what is the bottom line; exactly how he wants the judge to rule.

Joseph has ruled that Benjamin shall be retained as Joseph's slave (v. 17). Judah prays that he may be substituted for his youngest brother. Judah asks to take on Benjamin's punishment and that the boy be allowed to return to his father (v. 33). Judah gives two reasons for the prayer. His substitution will spare the old man sorrow. Second, Judah assumed a contractual duty to carry out any obligations on behalf of Benjamin when he pledged himself as surety for Benjamin's safe return (vv. 31–32) Joseph should now respect that contractual obligation. Both reasons turn on preserving the relationships within Jacob's family.

At the end of chapter 44 Judah has become a hopeless slave overtaken by unjust circumstances. He is crushed by the retributive justice system. The law demands punishment for past wrongs and offers no escape from the unjust accusation of theft. The consequence of Judah's sentence will be the total shredding of the social fabric that has held Jacob's family together. The condemnation of

Judah is an irreparable breach to which the law offers no remedy. All appears lost. The family is without resources. Figuratively, it is naked, in a pit in the wilderness without water.

Judah is in the same position as Joseph when he was thrown into prison in chapter 39, but there is a difference. The reader knows the Lord was with Joseph. Is that true for the wicked Judah who sold his brother into slavery and lay with his son's widow?

Restoration

Genesis 45:1–15

Then Joseph could no longer control himself before all
those who stood by him, and he cried out, 'Send everyone away from me.' So no one stayed with him when Joseph made himself known to his brothers. 2And he wept
so loudly that the Egyptians heard it, and the household
of Pharaoh heard it. 3Joseph said to his brothers, 'I am
Joseph. Is my father still alive?' But his brothers could
not answer him, so dismayed were they at his presence.
4 Then Joseph said to his brothers, 'Come closer to
me.' And they came closer. He said, 'I am your brother
Joseph, whom you sold into Egypt. 5And now do not be
distressed, or angry with yourselves, because you sold
me here; for God sent me before you to preserve life.
6For the famine has been in the land these two years;
and there are five more years in which there will be neither ploughing nor harvest. 7God sent me before you to
preserve for you a remnant on earth, and to keep alive
for you many survivors. 8So it was not you who sent
me here, but God; he has made me a father to Pharaoh,
and lord of all his house and ruler over all the land of
Egypt. 9Hurry and go up to my father and say to him,
"Thus says your son Joseph, God has made me lord of all
Egypt; come down to me, do not delay. 10You shall settle
in the land of Goshen, and you shall be near me, you
and your children and your children's children, as well
as your flocks, your herds, and all that you have. 11I will
provide for you there—since there are five more years of

> famine to come—so that you and your household, and
> all that you have, will not come to poverty." 12And now
> your eyes and the eyes of my brother Benjamin see that
> it is my own mouth that speaks to you. 13You must tell
> my father how greatly I am honoured in Egypt, and all
> that you have seen. Hurry and bring my father down
> here.' 14Then he fell upon his brother Benjamin's neck
> and wept, while Benjamin wept upon his neck. 15And
> he kissed all his brothers and wept upon them; and after
> that his brothers talked with him.

God's response to this quandary is given in the first 15 verses of chapter 45. As Tamar revealed the truth to Judah in chapter 38, so Joseph reveals the true nature of the situation to Judah and his brothers. The revelation is unexpected. The reader has no idea how God will re-establish the peace of Jacob's family. Again, Joseph weeps (v. 2). These are tears of joy. He reveals himself to his brothers (v. 3). The revelation is so extraordinary, beyond the ken of anything the brothers could even imagine, that the brothers react with dismay (v. 3). They are dumb struck.

Joseph explains God's intention. The explanation starts in verse 5 and begins with the word *now*. In Judah's side-bar the word *now* indicated his summation of his argument. In this case, Joseph is speaking on behalf of God who is the decision-maker and judge in this story. The "now" at the beginning of verse five is an indicator of what follows is the God's decision in this matter. In the modern judge's written opinion, this conclusion is usually indicated by the phrase "now therefore". What follows the "now" in verse 5 tells the reader God's answer to the question of what happens when humanity returns evil for good? How will God address humanity's overwhelming bias for error?

Three times in verses 5–8 Joseph repeats the phrase "God sent me before you." At this point, after the events in Joseph's life—the foretelling of the famine and the events during the brothers' time in Egypt—it is clear to the reader that God is the actor who controls what happens; God is the sovereign of the events related in the story of Jacob's family. God has sent Joseph to Egypt in order to preserve Jacob's family during the famine (v. 7). Joseph repeats

God's decision in verse 8, starting again with "now therefore". God sent Joseph to Egypt in order for him to become 'lord of all his [Pharaoh's] house and ruler over all the land of Egypt.' (v. 8). The repetition of the word *all* reminds the reader of the scope of Joseph's power under Pharaoh's order.

Joseph completely reframes the question raised by the prior events. The brothers thought events were controlled by retributive justice. They admitted they did wrong when they sold Joseph into slavery, and responded with distress and anger since they anticipated punishment (v. 5). This is the mindset of someone who has broken a contract. But the brothers misunderstood their transaction with the lord of the land. They thought it was simply a commercial transaction. Joseph points out that this mindset is wrong. Asking about a reckoning for past wrongs is not the real issue. The true issue is: what is God's intention? Joseph answers that question in his explanation. He explains that God sent Joseph to Egypt.

The brothers need not be troubled by guilt over their past misdeeds (v. 5). The retributive justice system focuses on what humanity does. If a person commits a wrong, then there is punishment. The system requires the person to act and then the law reacts. In Joseph's explanation, the focus is on what God intends. The story of Jacob's family puts God in charge.

The writer, through Joseph's explanation, is not extending mercy within the retributive justice system. Joseph is not forgiving his brothers' past wrongs. The verb for *forgive* is not in the text. Rather, the writer is addressing God's steadfast loyalty to Jacob's family. In spite of the obstacles created by humanity's wrongdoing, God continues to act for the benefit of Jacob's family. God's covenantal loyalty, his steadfast love, his lovingkindness (all translations of the Hebrew word *hesed*) is not deterred by past wrongs.

The wrongs set forth earlier in the story have impacted Jacob's family. There is no denying Joseph's anguish, but it does not deter God's steadfast loyalty. Jacob's family has failed in its loyalty to each other by these wrongs. It is only the Lord who shows steadfast loyalty. The writer does not raise the question of sin, or humanity's loyalty to God. What controls in the story of Jacob's family is God's intentions. God's steadfast love has the power of water, which always finds a way to flow on its intended path to the sea no matter what obstacles it encounters. God intends the preservation of Jacob's family

This trust in God's steadfast loyalty is outside the realm of justice. The attorney may understand the situation, but does not have the ultimate answer to the question of how humanity can go forward when hobbled by its overwhelming bias to error. The answer to the question of how to restore peace to Jacob's family, and by extension to all humanity, lies with God. This is the important lesson Joseph learned in captivity. His only hope is in God. That hope is now extended to all of Jacob's sons. God intends blessing, not retribution.

The brothers are saved by God from very specific threats. They are saved from a life of slavery. Joseph does not seek revenge under the retributive justice system. The iron grasp of the law's logic is broken. God has provided an alternative response to wrong doing. The brothers are saved from starving to death. The entire family faced ruin. God saved them from these real threats; not by promises of future happiness, but by providing the means for the family of Jacob to flourish in the present. This is God's blessing.

As an able administrator, Joseph does not linger on the theological understanding of past events, but swings into immediate action. Trusting in God's loving kindness, Joseph acts to make God's intentions a reality. The tone is set by the imperatives 'Hurry, and go up' (v. 9). This is another verbal coordination in Hebrew meaning "to go immediately, as fast as possible." Verse 9 ends with the order, 'do not delay.' The full order ends with the command, 'Hurry and bring my father down here.' (v. 13). Joseph wants no delay in restoring the family of Jacob. The irreparable breach caused by the brothers selling Joseph will be sewn up. God's steadfast loyalty makes a future possible.

The reunited family means the return to the good life described in Genesis 37:1–2. All Jacob's wealth will be preserved—children, children's children, flocks, herds— 'and all you have' (v. 10). This is abundant blessing. The family will be spared the hardship of the next five years of famine (v. 11). It is God's intention not only to restore the relationships in Jacob's family but also to assure the family's future well-being.

The revelation of Joseph's true identity and God's intentions for the family ends with kissing and weeping among the brothers (v. 15). For the moment, overwhelmed by the extraordinary revelation and outpouring of blessing, the brothers appear to be reconciled. Joseph has been restored from being a slave, a non-person, to being a man of great authority; his eleven brothers have been restored to Joseph with the prospect of a blessed future for the entire family.

Chapter 6

Family Reunion

WHILE JOSEPH AND HIS brothers are weeping and kissing, Jacob remains in Canaan awaiting restoration of his relationship with Joseph. The writer organizes this restoration around three orders or commands.

Pharaoh's Order

Genesis 45:16–28

[16] When the report was heard in Pharaoh's house, 'Joseph's
brothers have come', Pharaoh and his servants were
pleased. [17]Pharaoh said to Joseph, 'Say to your brothers,
"Do this: load your animals and go back to the land of
Canaan. [18]Take your father and your households and
come to me, so that I may give you the best of the land of
Egypt, and you may enjoy the fat of the land." [19]You are
further charged to say, "Do this: take wagons from the
land of Egypt for your little ones and for your wives, and
bring your father, and come. [20]Give no thought to your
possessions, for the best of all the land of Egypt is yours."'
[21] The sons of Israel did so. Joseph gave them wagons
according to the instruction of Pharaoh, and he gave
them provisions for the journey. [22]To each one of them
he gave a set of garments; but to Benjamin he gave three

> hundred pieces of silver and five sets of garments. [23]To
> his father he sent the following: ten donkeys loaded with the good things of Egypt, and ten female donkeys loaded with grain, bread, and provision for his father on the
> journey. [24]Then he sent his brothers on their way, and as they were leaving he said to them, 'Do not quarrel along the way.'
>
> [25] So they went up out of Egypt and came to their
> father Jacob in the land of Canaan. [26]And they told him,
> 'Joseph is still alive! He is even ruler over all the land of
> Egypt.' He was stunned; he could not believe them. [27]But
> when they told him all the words of Joseph that he had said to them, and when he saw the wagons that Joseph had sent to carry him, the spirit of their father Jacob re-
> vived. [28]Israel said, 'Enough! My son Joseph is still alive.
> I must go and see him before I die.'

The first command comes from Pharaoh. When Joseph revealed himself to his brothers, "he wept so loudly that the Egyptians heard it, and the household of Pharaoh heard it" (45:2). It is then reported to Pharaoh that his chief minister's brothers have been found (v. 16). "Pharaoh and his servants were pleased" (v. 16). A spirit of joy enters the narrative. Previously the brothers trembled with fear. When God's intentions are revealed, everyone, including the Egyptians, are pleased.

Pharaoh's initially speaks to Joseph, 'Say to your brothers' (v, 17); then in the next three verses there follow nine imperative verbs addressed to the brothers. *Do* this; *load* your animals; *go* back (this is shown by two imperatives in Hebrew); *take* your father (vv. 17–18). As a good commander, Pharaoh not only gives a precise order but also explains the order's goal. The order is intended to carry out Pharaoh's wish to give Joseph's family the best Egyptian land, in order that the family "may enjoy [imperative verb *eat* in Hebrew] the fat of the land" (v. 18). The initial order is expanded with further details. The order is authoritative, "*Do* this" (v. 19). The ninth imperative is: *take* wagons (v. 19), which is followed by two future actions in Hebrew which I would translate: thus you shall bring your father and you shall come (v. 19). Pharaoh's lavish intentions are summarized, 'for the best of all the land of Egypt is yours' (v. 20). Like both Potiphar, and the Prison Warden, Pharaoh shows unlimited trust in Joseph, and there are no limits to his generosity. The writer does not try to justify this generosity. Everyone accepts the windfall.

The order is carried out; the sons of Jacob obey (v. 21). Joseph implements the order. Benjamin and Jacob are given preferential treatment; their provisions are set out in detail, five sets of garments, ten female donkeys, and more (vv. 22–23). The reader sees evidence of Joseph's generosity.

As the brothers begin their mission to carry out Pharaoh's order, Joseph cautions them, 'Do not quarrel along the way' (v. 24). Joseph understands his brothers' true nature. While there was crying and kissing when the brothers were restored to Joseph (v. 15), this was not the beginning of a perfect reconciliation. Joseph's caution is similar to the writer's observation that Judah did not lie with Tamar after her restoration to Judah's household (38:26). The remedy for the breach caused by the brothers is not perfect; the family has been given a way forward that will allow them to survive the famine. The brothers have yet to show their full acceptance of Joseph as their superior. There remain many issues to be sorted out. The question implied in chapter 37 remains unanswered: Who will inherit Jacob's wealth? Joseph's caution is well placed. His brothers have a history of acting contrary to God's will. Will the brothers be at peace with the new arrangement?

The result of Pharaoh's order is that the brothers, once again, return to Jacob in Canaan and report on their adventures. In chapter 37, the brothers reported to Jacob on the loss of Joseph at Dothan. (37:32–35). In chapter 42, they report to their father on the complications arising from their first trip to Egypt (42:29–38). In both cases, Jacob is dismayed by the reports and foretells of his descent in sorrow to Sheol. In chapter 45, the brothers bring joy to their father with the news, 'Joseph is still alive!' (v. 26). After the shock of the news wears off, "the spirit of . . . Jacob revived" (v. 27). Based on the earlier reports, Jacob has every reason to question the truth of his sons' third report. It is only when he sees the physical evidence, the wagons sent by Joseph, which corroborates their story, that he accepts the truth of the matter (v. 27). Jacob responds by foreseeing a joyful reunion before he dies. There is no more talk of sorrow and Sheol.

God's Order

So far, the writer has suggested that Jacob's restoration with Joseph will be the work of Pharaoh. The reader may question this assumption in light of God's unique actions to restore Joseph in chapter 41, and his unique action in chapter 45 to restore the brothers to Joseph. The second order in chapter 46 further clarifies for the readers what is happening. It is God who is acting to restore Jacob to his beloved son.

> Genesis 46:1–4
>
> When Israel set out on his journey with all that he had
> and came to Beer-sheba, he offered sacrifices to the God
> of his father Isaac. [2]God spoke to Israel in visions of the
> night, and said, 'Jacob, Jacob.' And he said, 'Here I am.'
> [3]Then he said, 'I am God, the God of your father; do not
> be afraid to go down to Egypt, for I will make of you a
> great nation there. [4]I myself will go down with you to
> Egypt, and I will also bring you up again; and Joseph's
> own hand shall close your eyes.'

As Jacob sets out on his journey to Egypt, he comes to Beer-sheba. Previously at Beer-sheba, God ordered Isaac, Jacob's father, to stay out of Egypt (see Gen. 26:2–5) In this chapter, Jacob is encouraged to go down into Egypt (vv. 3–4).

God speaks to Jacob "in visions of the night" (v. 2). These visions are not like the dreams Joseph interpreted. In those dreams, an event which was described; for example, the sheaf arose and the ten sheaves bowed down, or the baker's cakes were eaten from his basket, or seven sleek and fat cows came up from the Nile. The events described in those dreams are ambiguous, and an interpreter is required to determine their meaning.

In Jacob's visions, there is no action. God speaks directly to Jacob and gives permission to go down to Egypt (v. 3). God does not use the imperative but rather tells Jacob, 'do not be afraid to go down to Egypt' (v. 3). These visions are an expansion of Jacob's vision at Luz / Bethel where "God said to him [Jacob/Israel] 'I am God Almighty: be fruitful and multiply; a nation and a company of nations shall come from you, and kings shall spring from you. The land that I gave to Abraham and Isaac I will give to you and I will give the land to your offspring after you'" (35:11–12).

In verse 3, God makes three statements to Jacob. First, God establishes his authority, 'I am God'; second, God encourages Jacob to move forward, 'do not be afraid to go down to Egypt'; and third, God will make a great nation of Jacob's family in Egypt. It is clear that God will bring these events to pass. '*I* will make of you a great nation there' (v. 3) [emphasis added].

In verse 4 God sets out three events that will occur. I myself will go down. I myself [the independent personal pronoun is repeated in the Hebrew text] will also bring you up (v. 4). The two repetitions of the independent personal pronoun, translated by the word *myself*, emphasize that it is God who is acting. These events are under God's sole control. The promise at Luz / Bethel will be fulfilled by going to Egypt. Finally, there is the promise that Jacob will have a good death: 'Joseph's own hand shall close your eyes' (v. 4). After twice predicting his own descent in sorrow to Sheol, Jacob now understands that peace awaits him at the end of his life.

These statements in verses three and four describe future events that are under God's control. They describe uncompleted actions, translated in English by the future tense, action which God *will* bring about. There can be no question that God controls the ultimate meaning of events in this story. God has no need to use the imperative with its subtle possibility that the imperative command will not be obeyed. What God has spoken will come about.

Genesis 46:5–30

5 Then Jacob set out from Beer-sheba; and the sons of Israel carried their father Jacob, their little ones, and their wives in the wagons that Pharaoh had sent to carry him. 6They also took their livestock and the goods that they had acquired in the land of Canaan, and they came into Egypt, Jacob and all his offspring with him, 7his sons, and his sons' sons with him, his daughters, and his sons' daughters; all his offspring he brought with him into Egypt.

8 Now these are the names of the Israelites, Jacob and his offspring, who came to Egypt. Reuben, Jacob's firstborn, 9and the children of Reuben: Hanoch, Pallu, Hezron, and Carmi. 10The children of Simeon: Jemuel, Jamin, Ohad, Jachin, Zohar, and Shaul, the son of a Canaanite woman. 11The children of Levi: Gershon, Kohath, and Merari. 12The children of Judah: Er, Onan, Shelah, Perez, and Zerah (but Er and Onan died in the land of Canaan); and the children of Perez were Hezron and Hamul. 13The children of Issachar: Tola, Puvah, Jashub, and Shimron. 14The children of Zebulun: Sered, Elon, and Jahleel 15(these are the sons of Leah, whom she bore to Jacob in Paddan-aram, together with his daughter Dinah; in all his sons and his daughters numbered thirty-three). 16The children of Gad: Ziphion, Haggi, Shuni, Ezbon, Eri, Arodi, and Areli. 17The children of Asher: Imnah, Ishvah, Ishvi, Beriah, and their sister Serah. The children of Beriah: Heber and Malchiel 18(these are the children of Zilpah, whom Laban gave to his daughter Leah; and these she bore to Jacob—sixteen persons). 19The children of Jacob's wife Rachel: Joseph and Benjamin. 20To Joseph in the land of Egypt were born Manasseh and Ephraim, whom Asenath daughter of Potiphera, priest of On, bore to him. 21The children of Benjamin: Bela, Becher, Ashbel, Gera, Naaman, Ehi, Rosh, Muppim, Huppim, and Ard 22(these are the children of Rachel, who were born to Jacob—fourteen persons in all). 23The children of Dan: Hashum. 24The children of Naphtali: Jahzeel, Guni, Jezer, and Shillem 25(these are the children of Bilhah, whom Laban gave to his daughter Rachel, and these she bore to Jacob—seven persons in all). 26All the persons belonging to Jacob who came into Egypt, who were his

> own offspring, not including the wives of his sons, were
> sixty-six persons in all. [27]The children of Joseph, who
> were born to him in Egypt, were two; all the persons of
> the house of Jacob who came into Egypt were seventy.
> [28] Israel sent Judah ahead to Joseph to lead the way
> before him into Goshen. When they came to the land of
> Goshen, [29]Joseph made ready his chariot and went up to
> meet his father Israel in Goshen. He presented himself
> to him, fell on his neck, and wept on his neck a good
> while. [30]Israel said to Joseph, 'I can die now, having seen
> for myself that you are still alive.'

Jacob and his sons carry out the Lord's plan. Everyone, the phrase "all his offspring" is repeated for emphasis, is saved from the famine. Everyone goes down to Egypt. No distinction is made between men and women; no distinction is made between adult and child. (vv. 5–7) To make this perfectly clear the writer sets out the name of each son and his children on the trip to Egypt (vv. 8–25). The ineffectual Reuben is listed. The naughty sons, Dan, Naphtali, Gad and Asher, are included (see 37:2). The record is clear; all are saved without qualification and without distinction. Not only is everyone saved, but all of Jacob's wealth is also saved (v. 6).

As a result of God's order, Joseph is restored to Jacob. There are abundant tears of joy (v. 29). The dream of the spangled heavens bowing to Joseph, told in Genesis 37:9–10 has been fulfilled. Jacob summarizes the reunion saying, 'I can die now, having seen for myself that you are still alive' (v. 30).

The Third Order

Genesis 46:31—47:12

> [31]Joseph said to his brothers and to his father's house-
> hold, 'I will go up and tell Pharaoh, and will say to him,
> "My brothers and my father's household, who were in the
> land of Canaan, have come to me. [32]The men are shep-
> herds, for they have been keepers of livestock; and they
> have brought their flocks, and their herds, and all that

> they have." [33]When Pharaoh calls you, and says, "What is your occupation?" [34]you shall say, "Your servants have been keepers of livestock from our youth even until now, both we and our ancestors"—in order that you may settle in the land of Goshen, because all shepherds are abhorrent to the Egyptians.'
>
> So Joseph went and told Pharaoh, 'My father and my brothers, with their flocks and herds and all that they possess, have come from the land of Canaan; they are now in the land of Goshen.' [2]From among his brothers he took five men and presented them to Pharaoh. [3]Pharaoh said to his brothers, 'What is your occupation?' And they said to Pharaoh, 'Your servants are shepherds, as our ancestors were.' [4]They said to Pharaoh, 'We have come to reside as aliens in the land; for there is no pasture for your servants' flocks because the famine is severe in the land of Canaan. Now, we ask you, let your servants settle in the land of Goshen.' [5]Then Pharaoh said to Joseph, 'Your father and your brothers have come to you. [6]The land of Egypt is before you; settle your father and your brothers in the best part of the land; let them live in the land of Goshen; and if you know that there are capable men among them, put them in charge of my livestock.'
>
> [7] Then Joseph brought in his father Jacob, and presented him before Pharaoh, and Jacob blessed Pharaoh. [8]Pharaoh said to Jacob, 'How many are the years of your life?' [9]Jacob said to Pharaoh, 'The years of my earthly sojourn are one hundred and thirty; few and hard have been the years of my life. They do not compare with the years of the life of my ancestors during their long sojourn.' [10]Then Jacob blessed Pharaoh, and went out from the presence of Pharaoh. [11]Joseph settled his father and his brothers, and granted them a holding in the land of Egypt, in the best part of the land, in the land of Rameses, as Pharaoh had instructed. [12]And Joseph provided his father, his brothers, and all his father's household with food, according to the number of their dependents.

Joseph, after the reunion, seeks to control the narrative that Pharaoh will be told. Joseph, with his experience in the Egyptian court, may not be entirely confident in Pharaoh's good will towards his family. Pharaoh acted on a whim with his chief cupbearer and baker. Being steadfastly loyal is not in Pharaoh's character. Joseph has thought out how he will present his family's case to Pharaoh. The plan starts with Joseph reporting that his family has arrived (v. 31). He will further specify that the Hebrews are experienced shepherds (v. 34). They have, moreover, brought their livestock with them (v. 32).

Joseph coaches his witnesses. He tells his brothers that Pharaoh will ask the question, 'What is your occupation?' (v. 33). He then feeds them the acceptable answer: 'you shall say, "Your servants have been keepers of livestock . . ."' (v. 34). Joseph is "wood shedding" his witnesses in preparation for their questioning by Pharaoh. The verb "to wood shed," as used by lawyers, suggests the attorney is metaphorically beating the answer into her witness. The precise answer the brothers are to give is important 'because all shepherds are abhorrent to the Egyptians' (v. 34). The new immigrants will not be taking jobs from the native Egyptians, but they will be doing necessary work that no Egyptian would undertake. Joseph's advice to his brothers gives the family the best chance to settle in Egypt and take advantage of the grasslands in Goshen.

Joseph goes before Pharaoh and reports that Pharaoh's order has been carried out. Joseph's entire family and all their possessions have arrived in Egypt (47:1). Joseph brings with him five of his brothers. Joseph has cherry-picked his corroborating witnesses. One can assume he chose his most intelligent brothers, the ones who understood the importance of their testimony and would stay on message. Reuben, for example, was probably not given the opportunity to prove himself, once again, to be ineffectual. This careful staging of the Hebrews' presentation before Pharaoh leads the reader to suspect that the outcome of the meeting is not a sure bet.

Pharaoh asks the expected question, and the brothers give the prepared response (v. 3). They then go off brief, as all witnesses are wont to do. They explain that they are only requesting refugee status in Egypt. Their migration has been forced upon them by the famine because 'there is no pasture' in their native land (v. 4).

The sons of Jacob are economic refugees. Then as good advocates, the chosen five conclude their presentation with a prayer, asking Pharaoh to enter a specific judgment: 'Now, we ask you, let your servants settle in the land of Goshen' (v. 4).

Pharaoh gives the requested order. "Settle [Hebrew imperative] your father and your brothers in the best part of the land; let them live in the land of Goshen' (v. 6). The third order completes the restoration of Joseph and Jacob. Joseph is reunited with his entire family in Egypt. They will not only have the means to survive the famine but will also flourish.

Jacob then enters Pharaoh's presence and blesses Pharaoh (vv. 7 and 10). Jacob's free ranging response to Pharaoh's question suggests Joseph did not "wood shed" his father. The promises Joseph makes in chapter 45:9–11, when he was first reunited with his brothers, have been fulfilled. The entire family settles in Goshen and Joseph provides for everyone (v. 12).

Three Deaths

Chapter 7

The Death of Egyptian Freedom

The well-being of Jacob's family, which was shattered by the brothers' betrayal of Joseph, is restored when the Hebrews arrive lock, stock, and barrel in the land of Goshen. The family has land and food which will assure their future (47:27). The writer turns in the final chapters of the story to address three deaths that conclude this story.

Genesis 47:13-28

[13] Now there was no food in all the land, for the famine
was very severe. The land of Egypt and the land of
Canaan languished because of the famine. [14]Joseph collected all the money to be found in the land of Egypt
and in the land of Canaan, in exchange for the grain that
they bought; and Joseph brought the money into Pharaoh's house. [15]When the money from the land of Egypt
and from the land of Canaan was spent, all the Egyptians
came to Joseph, and said, 'Give us food! Why should we
die before your eyes? For our money is gone.' [16]And Joseph answered, 'Give me your livestock, and I will give
you food in exchange for your livestock, if your money
is gone.' [17]So they brought their livestock to Joseph; and
Joseph gave them food in exchange for the horses, the
flocks, the herds, and the donkeys. That year he supplied
them with food in exchange for all their livestock. [18]When
that year was ended, they came to him the following year,

and said to him, 'We cannot hide from my lord that our
money is all spent; and the herds of cattle are my lord's.
There is nothing left in the sight of my lord but our bod-
ies and our lands. [19]Shall we die before your eyes, both we
and our land? Buy us and our land in exchange for food.
We with our land will become slaves to Pharaoh; just give
us seed, so that we may live and not die, and that the land
may not become desolate.'

[20] So Joseph bought all the land of Egypt for Pharaoh.
All the Egyptians sold their fields, because the famine
was severe upon them; and the land became Pharaoh's.
[21]As for the people, he made slaves of them from one end
of Egypt to the other. [22]Only the land of the priests he
did not buy; for the priests had a fixed allowance from
Pharaoh, and lived on the allowance that Pharaoh gave
them; therefore they did not sell their land. [23]Then Joseph said to the people, 'Now that I have this day bought
you and your land for Pharaoh, here is seed for you; sow
the land. [24]And at the harvests you shall give one-fifth to
Pharaoh, and four-fifths shall be your own, as seed for
the field and as food for yourselves and your households,
and as food for your little ones.' [25]They said, 'You have
saved our lives; may it please my lord, we will be slaves
to Pharaoh.' [26]So Joseph made it a statute concerning
the land of Egypt, and it stands to this day, that Pharaoh
should have the fifth. The land of the priests alone did
not become Pharaoh's.

[27] Thus Israel settled in the land of Egypt, in the
region of Goshen; and they gained possessions in it, and
were fruitful and multiplied exceedingly. [28]Jacob lived
in the land of Egypt for seventeen years; so the days of
Jacob, the years of his life, were one hundred and forty-
seven years.

The writer starts his wrapping up the story by looking at the consequences of the famine for the lives of the Egyptians. The famine leads to a metaphorical death; the death of freedom in Egypt. The Egyptians, because of the want of food, are exploited and go from being a free people to becoming slaves.

The reader is told in Genesis 41:56 that Joseph sold food to the Egyptian population during the famine. This is patently unjust, since the food in storage came from a tax paid by the Egyptians during the years of abundance. The modern understanding of taxes is that the funds raised are for the general welfare, not the enrichment of the sovereign. In Joseph's time, the taxes collected are the property of Pharaoh and for his benefit.

In Genesis 47:13–28, the writer examines the consequences of this policy more carefully. It is a study of power and the consequences of the unfettered market place. The crisis turns on the law of supply and demand. Pharaoh has the only supply of food, and the population is demanding relief from the famine. There is no counter balance to Pharaoh's economic superiority. God does not appear to be present in this section of narrative.

The context of the problem is set out in verse 13. The famine is severe and there is no food (v. 13). In the first stage, Joseph sells food, which he has stored as a result of Pharaoh's dream, foretelling a severe famine in the land. The sale to the general population is in exchange for money (v. 14). Joseph is assiduous in carrying out his duty as the overseer of Pharaoh's property; the food belongs to Pharaoh and not Joseph. Joseph himself has nothing to give away. The money is turned over to Pharaoh. This arrangement turns on Joseph's respect for his fiduciary duty, a respect that Joseph has already shown in his work for Potiphar.

When the money runs out, Joseph demands livestock in exchange for food (v. 17). This is not an arms-length commercial transaction, in contrast to the negotiations between Judah and Tamar. The people face starvation. 'Give us food! Why should we die before your eyes?' (v. 15). They have no choice but to comply with Joseph's demands. Joseph is exploiting them; taking advantage of their weakness.

In the third stage, the money is all spent and the livestock is all under Joseph's control (v. 18). The Egyptians then propose to sell themselves and their land to Joseph in exchange for food (v. 19). Joseph buys the land and the people become slaves (vv. 20–21). Joseph finishes by imposing a crop share rent on the land.

Twenty percent of the harvest is given to Pharaoh and the slaves are allowed to keep the rest (v. 24). The Egyptian people have been ruthlessly beaten down. The reader could rightly conclude that any gratitude expressed to Joseph was the coerced begging of people with little hope for the future (see v. 25).

The writer concludes this section, "Thus Israel settled in the land of Egypt, in the region of Goshen; and they gained possessions in it, and were fruitful and multiplied exceedingly" (v. 27). The contrast with the state of the starving Egyptians could not be more stark. Israel does not suffer during the famine.

The state of the Egyptian economy is a warning to the Israelites. When a people do not own the land and hard times come, as they inevitably do, the people may lose their freedom and become slaves in order to survive. The brothers' greatest fear in their second encounter with Joseph was that they would be overpowered and made slaves (Gen. 43:18). That dreaded situation almost befalls the brothers during their third encounter with Joseph in chapter 44. This passage concerning the fate of the Egyptians shows the Hebrews what can happen if they do not own their land and remain merely sojourners in the land. The nightmare of slavery is a real possibility for people who are not a nation with their own land. The Hebrews have received God's promise that he will give them the land of Canaan as their possession (48:3). The fulfillment of that promise will allow the Hebrews to avoid the situation of the Egyptians under the control of Joseph.

This turn of events points the reader forward. It suggests a strong justification for the Egyptians' future policy of making Hebrews slaves in Egypt, as narrated in the book of Exodus. The Hebrews set themselves up as a foreign elite who live apart and thus become the subject of envy among the native population.

Finally, the passage reminds the reader that an unfettered market place with unrestrained economic forces leads to disaster. Unrestrained human power leads to exploitation. No one and nothing stopped Pharaoh from hanging his chief baker. In Egypt, Joseph's coercion of payments from a starving population show that the assiduous application of the law of supply and demand does not assure the well-being of a people. The events in Joseph's life suggest the reader must look to God's steadfast love for deliverance, as a force to counter balance the despot Pharaoh and economic exploitation.

Chapter 8

The Death of Jacob

Genesis 47:29–31

[29] When the time of Israel's death drew near, he called
his son Joseph and said to him, 'If I have found favour
with you, put your hand under my thigh and promise to
deal loyally and truly with me. Do not bury me in Egypt.
30When I lie down with my ancestors, carry me out of
Egypt and bury me in their burial place.' He answered, 'I
will do as you have said.' 31And he said, 'Swear to me';
and he swore to him. Then Israel bowed himself on the
head of his bed.

THIS PASSAGE SETS OUT the events leading up to Jacob's death. Jacob has three death-bed wishes. This is Jacob's estate plan. This plan will answer the questions raised in the first chapter: Who will inherit Jacob's property? Who will be the chosen one with whom God will make his covenant? Jacob's estate plan will confirm whether the brothers' jealousy was valid.

The first passage foretells Jacob's death; "the time of Israel's death drew near" (v. 29). Jacob remains firmly in control and will not leave the arrangements for his death to chance. Joseph is summoned (v. 29). Jacob does not want to be buried in Egypt. He wants to be buried with his ancestors in their burial place in Canaan (v.

30). Jacob will expand on the importance of this wish in his final words to his sons (see 49:29–32).

To assure that this wish will be carried out, Jacob requires Joseph to swear an oath promising that he will do as Jacob has said (v. 31). The solemnity of the oath is established by the manner of oath taking, 'put your hand under my thigh.' This is the established method for taking an oath at the time of the patriarchs. Abraham required the same ritual when taking an oath from his servant in Genesis 24:2. Jacob is placing a categorical duty on his son, the verb "to swear" is repeated for emphasis.

The standard by which Joseph is to carry out his duties is the absolute highest. He is to deal with Jacob with loyalty and truth (v. 29). The Hebrew text uses two nouns for one concept. The first noun is *hesed*, "loyalty," and the second is *emes,* "truth." The second noun, "truth," modifies the first noun, "loyalty." Williams suggests a possible translation, "true loyalty?".[18] The noun *hesed* was previously used by the writer to describe the God's presence with Joseph. Genesis 39:21 states that God showed Joseph steadfast love, and the word used is *hesed.* The loyalty being shown arises in a relationship. The word can be translated "covenantal loyalty," thus emphasizing that the loyalty arises in a relationship. Jacob has required Joseph to act as God would, at the highest level of loyalty.

> Genesis 48:1–22
>
> After this Joseph was told, 'Your father is ill.' So he took
> with him his two sons Manasseh and Ephraim. [2]When
> Jacob was told, 'Your son Joseph has come to you,' he
> summoned his strength and sat up in bed. [3]And Jacob
> said to Joseph, 'God Almighty appeared to me at Luz in
> the land of Canaan, and he blessed me, [4]and said to me,
> "I am going to make you fruitful and increase your num-
> bers; I will make of you a company of peoples, and will
> give this land to your offspring after you for a perpetual
> holding." [5]Therefore your two sons, who were born to

18. Ronald J. Williams, *Williams' Hebrew Syntax, Third Edition, Revised and Expanded by John C. Beckman* (Toronto: University of Toronto Press, 2007), section 72, p. 20.

you in the land of Egypt before I came to you in Egypt,
are now mine; Ephraim and Manasseh shall be mine, just
as Reuben and Simeon are. 6As for the offspring born to
you after them, they shall be yours. They shall be recorded under the names of their brothers with regard to their
inheritance. 7For when I came from Paddan, Rachel, alas,
died in the land of Canaan on the way, while there was
still some distance to go to Ephrath; and I buried her
there on the way to Ephrath' (that is, Bethlehem).

8 When Israel saw Joseph's sons, he said, 'Who are
these?' 9Joseph said to his father, 'They are my sons,
whom God has given me here.' And he said, 'Bring them
to me, please, that I may bless them.' 10Now the eyes of
Israel were dim with age, and he could not see well. So
Joseph brought them near him; and he kissed them and
embraced them. 11Israel said to Joseph, 'I did not expect
to see your face; and here God has let me see your children also.' 12Then Joseph removed them from his father's
knees, and he bowed himself with his face to the earth.
13Joseph took them both, Ephraim in his right hand towards Israel's left, and Manasseh in his left hand towards
Israel's right, and brought them near him. 14But Israel
stretched out his right hand and laid it on the head of
Ephraim, who was the younger, and his left hand on the
head of Manasseh, crossing his hands, for Manasseh was
the firstborn. 15He blessed Joseph, and said, 'The God before whom my ancestors Abraham and Isaac walked, the
God who has been my shepherd all my life to this day, 16
the angel who has redeemed me from all harm, bless the
boys; and in them let my name be perpetuated, and the
name of my ancestors Abraham and Isaac; and let them
grow into a multitude on the earth.'

17 When Joseph saw that his father laid his right
hand on the head of Ephraim, it displeased him; so he
took his father's hand, to remove it from Ephraim's head
to Manasseh's head. 18Joseph said to his father, 'Not so,
my father! Since this one is the firstborn, put your right
hand on his head.' 19But his father refused, and said, 'I
know, my son, I know; he also shall become a people, and
he also shall be great. Nevertheless, his younger brother
shall be greater than he, and his offspring shall become

> a multitude of nations.' [20]So he blessed them that day, saying, 'By you Israel will invoke blessings, saying, "God make you like Ephraim and like Manasseh."' So he put Ephraim ahead of Manasseh. [21]Then Israel said to Joseph, 'I am about to die, but God will be with you and will bring you again to the land of your ancestors. [22]I now give to you one portion more than to your brothers, the portion that I took from the hand of the Amorites with my sword and with my bow.'

Having addressed his most pressing concern, Jacob turns his attention to assuring Joseph's special status among Jacob's sons. Joseph presents his two sons to be blessed by his father (48:1). Jacob starts by reviewing God Almighty's promise at Luz (v. 3). There is an interesting divergence in the direction of his argument. Jacob declares that Joseph's two sons will be considered his direct heirs along with Jacob's other sons, Reuben and Simeon (v. 5). Jacob appears to argue that his beloved wife Rachel, mother of Joseph and Benjamin, died prematurely. The two sons of Joseph, Ephraim and Manasseh, will, therefore, take the place of the sons Jacob believes he would have fathered with Rachel if she had not died before her time on route to the land of Canaan (v. 7).

The basis of Jacob's reasoning escapes the modern reader. This shift in his argument is made without putting in the clutch. No one is assured of future children or their survival. But the outcome of Jacob's adoption is clear. Joseph's family gets a double portion of Jacob's inheritance. In a *per stirpes* [by representation] distribution of assets, the children take the portion that would have been their father's. Under this system, Ephraim and Manasseh would each get a half of Joseph's whole share, as the representatives of their father. But Jacob has elevated the status of Joseph's sons to a *per capita* [by head] level of distribution. Under Jacob's estate plan, Ephraim and Manasseh will take the same share as Jacob's other sons, they are counted among Jacob's sons, not as Joseph's sons, effective doubling the share for Joseph's family.

Jacob next turns his attention to the two boys whom he will bless (v. 9). Jacob recalls his amazement that he has been reunited with Joseph and his even greater wonder that he has lived to see Joseph's two sons (v. 11).

The boys initially sit on Jacob's knee and Jacob kisses and hugs them (v. 10). Joseph then takes the boys back and as an able administrator, prepares the boys to be blessed. Joseph holds the youngest boy, Ephraim, in his right hand. They are facing Jacob. Ephraim is, opposite Jacob's left hand. Manasseh, the oldest boy is in Joseph's left hand, opposite Jacob's right hand (v. 13). The right hand of Jacob is the preferred position, the one with greater power. All that is required of Jacob is to stretch out his hands straight in front of him and bless the boys, thus respecting their birth order.

Jacob in his dotage wrests control of the situation away from Joseph. He crosses his arms, giving the greater blessing to the younger Ephraim, and thus displacing the expected position of Manasseh, the elder (v. 14). While shocking to Joseph, the gesture is not without precedent. Isaac was chosen over the older son, Ishmael; Jacob displaced his older brother Esau; Joseph is favored over his older brothers; Perez will become greater than the first born Zerah. Throughout the book of Genesis the expectation of who will be favored is upset.

Joseph, the able administrator, is "displeased" by this change in the protocol (v. 17). He tries to reassert his control of the situation, taking his feeble father's hand "to remove it from Ephraim's head to Manasseh's head" (v. 17). While Joseph may not have "wood shedded" his father in preparation for his presentation before Pharaoh, Joseph is not above some aggressive self-help to make things go his way. Jacob will have none of it; he puts "Ephraim ahead of Manasseh" (v. 20). Interestingly in the blessing of Joseph's children, it is Jacob who carries out God's will, and Joseph, who is often the spokesperson for God, fails to understand what God intends. The hero of our story is not perfect.

Jacob affirms his testamentary intent as reflected in the blessing of Joseph's sons. Joseph will receive one portion more than his brothers (v. 22). Joseph receives the share ordinarily reserved for the oldest son.

The Death of Jacob

Genesis 49:1–33

Then Jacob called his sons, and said: ‘Gather around, that I may tell you what will happen to you in days to come. [2] Assemble and hear, O sons of Jacob; listen to Israel your father.

[3] ‘Reuben, you are my firstborn, my might and the first fruits of my vigour, excelling in rank and excelling in power. [4] Unstable as water, you shall no longer excel because you went up on to your father’s bed; then you defiled it—you went up on to my couch!

[5] ‘Simeon and Levi are brothers; weapons of violence are their swords. [6] May I never come into their council; may I not be joined to their company—for in their anger they killed men, and at their whim they hamstrung oxen. [7] Cursed be their anger, for it is fierce, and their wrath, for it is cruel! I will divide them in Jacob, and scatter them in Israel.

[8] ‘Judah, your brothers shall praise you; your hand shall be on the neck of your enemies; your father’s sons shall bow down before you. [9] Judah is a lion’s whelp; from the prey, my son, you have gone up. He crouches down, he stretches out like a lion, like a lioness—who dares rouse him up? [10] The sceptre shall not depart from Judah, nor the ruler’s staff from between his feet, until tribute comes to him; and the obedience of the peoples is his. [11] Binding his foal to the vine and his donkey’s colt to the choice vine, he washes his garments in wine and his robe in the blood of grapes; [12] his eyes are darker than wine, and his teeth whiter than milk.

[13] ‘Zebulun shall settle at the shore of the sea; he shall be a haven for ships, and his border shall be at Sidon.

[14] ‘Issachar is a strong donkey, lying down between the sheepfolds; [15] he saw that a resting-place was good, and that the land was pleasant; so he bowed his shoulder to the burden, and became a slave at forced labour.

[16] ‘Dan shall judge his people as one of the tribes of Israel. [17] Dan shall be a snake by the roadside, a viper along the path, that bites the horse’s heels so that its rider falls backwards.

[18] ‘I wait for your salvation, O Lord.

> 19 'Gad shall be raided by raiders, but he shall raid at their heels.
>
> 20 'Asher's food shall be rich, and he shall provide royal delicacies.
>
> 21 'Naphtali is a doe let loose that bears lovely fawns.
>
> 22 'Joseph is a fruitful bough, a fruitful bough by a spring; his branches run over the wall. 23 The archers fiercely attacked him; they shot at him and pressed him hard. 24 Yet his bow remained taut, and his arms were made agile by the hands of the Mighty One of Jacob, by the name of the Shepherd, the Rock of Israel, 25 by the God of your father, who will help you, by the Almighty who will bless you with blessings of heaven above, blessings of the deep that lies beneath, blessings of the breasts and of the womb. 26 The blessings of your father are stronger than the blessings of the eternal mountains, the bounties of the everlasting hills; may they be on the head of Joseph, on the brow of him who was set apart from his brothers.
>
> 27 'Benjamin is a ravenous wolf, in the morning devouring the prey, and at evening dividing the spoil.'
>
> 28 All these are the twelve tribes of Israel, and this is what their father said to them when he blessed them, blessing each one of them with a suitable blessing.
>
> 29 Then he charged them, saying to them, 'I am about to be gathered to my people. Bury me with my ancestors—in the cave in the field of Ephron the Hittite, 30 in the cave in the field at Machpelah, near Mamre, in the land of Canaan, in the field that Abraham bought from Ephron the Hittite as a burial site. 31 There Abraham and his wife Sarah were buried; there Isaac and his wife Rebekah were buried; and there I buried Leah— 32 the field and the cave that is in it were purchased from the Hittites.' 33 When Jacob ended his charge to his sons, he drew up his feet into the bed, breathed his last, and was gathered to his people.

Finally, Jacob puts into place his full estate plan. "All these, are the twelve tribes of Israel, and this is what their father said to them when he blessed them, blessing each one of them with a suitable blessing" (49:28). Everyone gets his fair share. Everyone gets a share of Jacob's inheritance. There are no winners and losers. Jacob provides for all and by extension, the reader can conclude that God's steadfast love is with everyone. There is no real cause for the jealousy expressed at the beginning of the story. The brothers, along with the reader, have been asking the wrong question. The issue is not who gets what; but rather the wonder of the Lord's abundant blessing that provides for all. The inclusiveness of the blessing is reinforced by specifically setting out the individual names of all twelve sons.

The individual blessings are hard to decipher. In the first blessing Reuben is described, 'Unstable as water, you shall no longer excel because you went up to your father's bed; then you defiled it—you went up on to my couch!" (v. 4). This reads like a story of incest rather than blessing (see Gen. 35:22). Whatever may have been the writer's intentions in these individual passages, he summarizes that Jacob's blessing was appropriate for each son (v. 28). Everyone is delivered from Canaan during the famine. Everyone, including the scapegrace Reuben, is blessed. There is no question of who merits the Lord's blessing or who by past wrongs is foreclosed from the Lord's blessing.

Once again, Jacob returns to the paramount issue for him; where he is to be buried. He charges all his sons with a duty (v. 29). Jacob requests to be buried with his ancestors. Place of burial is of the utmost importance. The reader knows that Rachel died prematurely and is buried at Bethlehem (48:7). At the end of his life, Jacob reviews the names of all his ancestors who are buried 'in a cave in the field at Machpelah, near Mamre, in the land of Canaan' (v. 30). The sons are admonished to bury him at this place. These are Jacob's last words (v. 33). Jacob has carried out his three-point estate plan: he has arranged for his proper burial, he has assured Joseph's preferential inheritance, and he confirms the Lord's blessing for all his sons.

Chapter 9

The Death of Joseph

THE FINAL PASSAGE OF the story concerns the aftermath of Jacob's death, a promise for the future and the death of Joseph. The lives of the first generation of Jacob's family are drawing to a close.

> Genesis 50:1–14
>
> Then Joseph threw himself on his father's face and wept
> over him and kissed him. [2]Joseph commanded the physi-
> cians in his service to embalm his father. So the physi-
> cians embalmed Israel; [3]they spent forty days in doing
> this, for that is the time required for embalming. And the
> Egyptians wept for him for seventy days.
>
> [4] When the days of weeping for him were past,
> Joseph addressed the household of Pharaoh, 'If now I
> have found favour with you, please speak to Pharaoh as
> follows: [5]My father made me swear an oath; he said, "I
> am about to die. In the tomb that I hewed out for myself
> in the land of Canaan, there you shall bury me." Now
> therefore let me go up, so that I may bury my father; then
> I will return.' [6]Pharaoh answered, 'Go up, and bury your
> father, as he made you swear to do.'
>
> [7] So Joseph went up to bury his father. With him
> went up all the servants of Pharaoh, the elders of his
> household, and all the elders of the land of Egypt, [8]as
> well as all the household of Joseph, his brothers, and his
> father's household. Only their children, their flocks, and

> their herds were left in the land of Goshen. 9 Both chari-
> ots and charioteers went up with him. It was a very great
> company. 10 When they came to the threshing-floor of
> Atad, which is beyond the Jordan, they held there a very
> great and sorrowful lamentation; and he observed a time
> of mourning for his father for seven days. 11 When the
> Canaanite inhabitants of the land saw the mourning on
> the threshing-floor of Atad, they said, 'This is a grievous
> mourning on the part of the Egyptians.' Therefore the
> place was named Abel-mizraim; it is beyond the Jordan.
> 12 Thus his sons did for him as he had instructed them.
> 13 They carried him to the land of Canaan and buried
> him in the cave of the field at Machpelah, the field near
> Mamre, which Abraham bought as a burial site from
> Ephron the Hittite. 14 After he had buried his father, Jo-
> seph returned to Egypt with his brothers and all who had
> gone up with him to bury his father.

In the first three chapters of the story, the writer looked at a variety of circumstances where a member of Jacob's family had a duty towards another family member and failed to carry out that duty. The brothers failed in their duty to protect Joseph; Judah failed in his duty to provide Tamar with a husband; Potiphar's wife tried to seduce Joseph into forgetting his duty to his master. In 50:1–14, Jacob's family assiduously carries out its duty to provide a proper burial for Jacob, the family's patriarch.

Joseph weeps over his father (50:1). These are tears of grief. Joseph then proceeds to organize the burial of Jacob in Canaan. He seeks permission from Pharaoh to temporarily leave Egypt in order to bury his father (v. 5). The oath Jacob made Joseph solemnly swear is important. It is repeated to Pharaoh (v. 5). Joseph's duty is clear. This mandatory obligation is the justification for Pharaoh granting permission to bury Jacob in Canaan (v. 6).

The obligation is carried out by everyone—all the servants of Pharaoh and the officials of Pharaoh's household, and all the household of Joseph, his brothers, and all of Jacob's household. To emphasize that the company was all inclusive, the writer then sets out a very narrow exception. "Only their children, their flocks, and their herds were left in the land of Goshen" (v. 8). Having specified an exception, the writer indicates that anyone or anything not named is included. The story summarizes, "It was a very great company" (v. 9).

This great host of people arrive at the burial site, the threshing-floor of Atad (v. 11). There, a great observance is held (v. 10). The company of mourners is so large and the observance so extraordinary that it captures the attention of the local inhabitants (v. 11); everyone knows that Jacob was a most important man.

The writer again repeats that Jacob's sons have fulfilled their duty to their father. "Thus the sons did for him [Jacob] as he had instructed them. They carried him to the land of Canaan and buried him in the cave in the field at Machpelah, the field near Mamre, which Abraham bought as a burial site from Ephron the Hittite" (vv. 12–13). The obligation is repeated in very specific detail. It is very important to the writer that the sons did as their father instructed. After many tales of wrong doing and misperception, the story concludes with the family of Jacob acting together to carry out their duty to their father.

> Genesis 50:15–21
>
> [15] Realizing that their father was dead, Joseph's brothers said, 'What if Joseph still bears a grudge against us and pays us back in full for all the wrong that we did to him?' [16]So they approached Joseph, saying, 'Your father gave this instruction before he died, [17]"Say to Joseph: I beg you, forgive the crime of your brothers and the wrong they did in harming you." Now therefore please forgive the crime of the servants of the God of your father.' Joseph wept when they spoke to him. [18]Then his brothers also wept, fell down before him, and said, 'We are here as your slaves.' [19]But Joseph said to them, 'Do not be afraid! Am I in the place of God? [20]Even though you intended to do harm to me, God intended it for good, in order to preserve a numerous people, as he is doing today. [21]So have no fear; I myself will provide for you and your little ones.' In this way he reassured them, speaking kindly to them.

With the death of Jacob, the position of family patriarch is empty. Joseph is in a position of supreme power, lord of the land, without Jacob's authority as a counter balance. His brothers are totally dependent on Joseph for their survival. Without Joseph's good will, the brothers and their entire households would become like the Egyptians during the famine, slaves to Pharaoh. The brothers are afraid.

Continuing to think in terms of a retributive justice system, Joseph's brothers set out their reasoning in a conditional sentence: 'What if Joseph still bears a grudge against us and [then] pays us back in full for all the wrong that we did to him?' (v. 15). The brothers fear that in the future Joseph will hand them their just desserts. They were disloyal to Joseph and anticipate that Joseph will forget his duty of loyalty to his family.

The translation for verse 16 reads, "So they approached Joseph, saying, 'Your father gave this instruction [*tsavah*] before he died'" (v. 16). The Hebrew word, *tsavah*, has been used several times in this passage. In his last words, Jacob *charged* his sons. (49:29), and again "Jacob ended his *charge* to his sons" (v. 33). After Jacob's death, Joseph "commanded [*charged*] the physicians" (50:2). The writer concludes, after Jacob's burial, "Thus his sons did for him as he had instructed [*charged*] them" (v. 12). These verses all use the word *tsavah*. The word is used to show that an order or obligation, a charge, is being placed on the direct object of the verb.

After the funeral, the brothers attempt to charge Joseph with one more duty. Everyone scrupulously obeyed their father's charge concerning his burial (vv. 4–14). Afterwards they seek to impose a mandatory obligation with similar weight on Joseph. The brothers want to exploit Joseph's grief and his strong sense of duty of loyalty to Jacob. They have no authority of their own to impose the duty, so they cloak their demand in their father's prerogative. They place the obligation in the mouth of their dead father. In a hierarchical society, a father's charge is law for the son, as shown in the burial ceremonies for Jacob. The brothers hope by this attempt at self-help to avoid Joseph's vengeance.

The reader may well suspect that this is all a lie. The unreal condition of the brothers' story is set out in verse 15 with the question, "What if Joseph still bears a grudge against us?". Furthermore, the brothers' statement is rank hearsay. The brothers are repeating what they allegedly heard Jacob say. Under the brothers' story, the authority for the duty lies with Jacob, who is dead and no longer available to explain his orders. The acceptable evidence of this duty would have been for Jacob to have expressed the idea before he died when everyone would have heard the charge. With hearsay, the court is unable to question the speaker and thus test the truth of the statement. The reader has repeatedly seen the necessity of cross-examining the brothers to determine the full truth.

As a rule, hearsay testimony is not considered by the court. Hearsay evidence is ripe for fraud. The brothers try to mislead Joseph with their story of what Jacob allegedly said, just as they misled their father when they set Joseph's bloody coat before Jacob. After all that has transpired in the life of Jacob's family, the brothers have not had a change of heart or amended their ways. They continue to disregard the truth.

The brothers attempt to exploit Joseph's grief just as he exploited the starving Egyptians. The brothers' false obligation would require Joseph to, 'forgive the crime of your brothers and the wrong they did in harming you' [allegedly quoting Jacob] (v. 17a). To make sure Joseph understands what is required of him, they end their pleading with a prayer that sets out exactly how they want Joseph to act: 'Now therefore please forgive the crime [rebellion] of the servants of the God of your father' (v. 17b).

The brothers are tying Joseph's forgiveness of their crimes with the forgiveness of their crime or sin. Effectively, Joseph would be the grantor of amnesty for sin. They are asking for mercy as an option in the retributive justice system. The brothers are still asking the wrong question: What will be the reckoning for our crimes? They have not advanced in their thinking beyond what they expressed in their first encounter with Joseph in chapter 42. 'Alas, we are paying the penalty for what we did to our brother; we saw his anguish when he pleaded with us, but we would not listen. That is why this anguish has come upon us' (42:21).

Furthermore, they have a wrong understanding of how the Lord deals with humanity; they make God's power to forgive dependent on Joseph's act of forgiveness. Joseph will have none of it; he weeps (v. 17). These must be tears of frustration. The brothers have failed to grasp that God is not bound by the retributive justice system. What controls is what God intends. Joseph explained this when he was first reunited with his brothers (45:7–8). God shows his goodwill towards Jacob's family by providing the family with abundant blessing. But the brothers have failed to grasp this basic concept. This failure also suggests that the brothers are not truly reconciled to Joseph as the head of the family. They continue after all these years to be afraid of Joseph.

The brothers also weep. Their tears, in all likelihood, are tears of self-pity. They fall down before Joseph and declare their utter abasement, 'We are here as your slaves' (v. 18). This is the second time the brothers are completely bereft of all hope. They are in the same position as Judah before Joseph reveals himself (see 44:33). The dream of the sheaves is again fulfilled (see 37:6–7).

Joseph answers his brothers with further assurances, as he did in Genesis 45. "Do not be afraid!" These are words of comfort. In 45:5 Joseph cautions the brothers not to be distressed or angry with yourselves. This is the categorical rejection of the application of retributive justice; the brothers will not receive their just desserts. "Do not be afraid" is a phrase used to indicate that the speaker is expressing the Lord's intention. The writer is reinforcing the idea that Joseph is acting as the spokesperson for the Lord and that he has a message of deliverance from the bounds of retributive justice.

Moreover, Joseph corrects their misperception of God's relationship with humanity. Joseph asks the question, "Am I in the place of God?" (v. 19). The clear answer is that Joseph does not act for God. He interprets God's intentions, as the reader saw in Joseph's interpretation of the three dreams, but he does not act in God's stead. The answer implies the understanding that only God can forgive sins. Joseph's forgiveness is irrelevant. Joseph never says the words, "I forgive you." Forgiveness is not an element in the story of Jacob's family. The power to forgive sins rests with the Lord alone and it does not come into play in this story.

Joseph repeats God's intentions. God sent Joseph to Egypt 'in order to preserve a numerous people' (v. 20). This is the same purpose that was set out in Genesis 45:7. The brothers may have intended harm to Joseph, but God rectified the situation and carried out his intentions, 'as he is doing today' (v. 20). The crucial point for the writer of the story, is that God's will is done. The brothers, like sheep, went astray, but the Shepherd of Israel led everyone safely home, to a place of well-being. Neither Joseph nor the writer is concerned with punishing those who went astray in the past.

Joseph finishes his assurances with a promise for the future. He uses the words that set out a judge's decision, "now therefore." 'I myself will provide for you and your little ones' (v. 21). God has preserved the entire family of Jacob; no one was cast aside or abandoned. Moreover, God's good will extends to future generations.

In Chapter 45:7, the Lord's saving act is described in the Hebrew text "by means of a great deliverance." The idea of deliverance is also translated by the word *escape*. The brothers have been given an escape from the dead end of their lives characterized by famine, slavery and family discord. This is reasserted in chapter 50. But the brothers have not been transformed by their deliverance. Like bad law students, they understand the judge's holding in their case, they know that they have been saved by God. They do not, however, understand the Lord's intentions. They fail to grasp the concepts of retributive justice are inapplicable to the God's dealing with humanity.

There is no evidence that anyone in the story praises God for his bountiful goodness, except Jacob who sacrifices to the God of his father at Beersheba (46:1), Yet, in spite of their wrong doing, in spite of their continued misperceptions and misunderstandings, in spite of their lack of response, the Lord remains steadfast in the goodwill towards his chosen people and continues to carry out his benevolent intentions for them. All are saved. All are blessed.

Genesis 50:22–26

[22] So Joseph remained in Egypt, he and his father's
household; and Joseph lived for one hundred and ten
years. [23]Joseph saw Ephraim's children of the third generation; the children of Machir son of Manasseh were
also born on Joseph's knees.
[24] Then Joseph said to his brothers, 'I am about to
die; but God will surely come to you, and bring you up
out of this land to the land that he swore to Abraham, to
Isaac, and to Jacob.' [25]So Joseph made the Israelites swear,
saying, 'When God comes to you, you shall carry up my
bones from here.' [26]And Joseph died, being one hundred
and ten years old; he was embalmed and placed in a cof-
fin in Egypt.

The story ends with the death of its hero Joseph, who lives into old age (v. 22) and sees Ephraim's children for three generations and the grandchildren of Manasseh (v. 23). As death approaches, Joseph reminds the Israelites that God has promised to give them the land he promised to Abraham, Isaac and Jacob (v. 24). This part of God's plan will be fulfilled after Joseph's death. This future fulfillment comes with a responsibility. Joseph's bones are to be preserved and carried back to the land of Canaan when the Israelites are delivered from Egypt (v. 25).

www.ingramcontent.com/pod-product-compliance
Lightning Source LLC
LaVergne TN
LVHW010932100826
845153LV00001B/10

* 9 7 8 1 5 3 2 6 3 9 3 8 8 *